LUXOR

A GUIDE TO THE TEMPLES & TOMBS OF ANCIENT THEBES

LUXOR

A Guide to the Temples & Tombs of Ancient Thebes

Ian Portman

THE AMERICAN UNIVERSITY IN CAIRO PRESS

Photographs for this book are by:
Jaroslaw Kosuch (pages 9,17,18,28-34,45-47,49,50,77,78)
Jasper Bouverie (pages 2,19,23,39,42,54,81,83,85)
Ted Brock (inside cover and pages 35,41,51-53,57,60,62-65,66,67)
Jean-Claude Aunos (front cover, and page 13)
Mahmoud Nour (pages 26,36)
Christine Marivin (pages 25,82)
Tawhid Ramy (pages 4 and 11)
and Liz Wickett (page 21)

The illustrations on pages 6,12,19,48,61,80 and 87 are by Jenny Leimert
The illustration on page 3 is by Salah Moustafa Ibrahim

The plans of the temples and tombs were drawn by Adel Zaki
The maps were made at The Palm Press
by Raouf Kamel Naguib and Nabil George

The book was designed by Ian Portman
Set in Palatino type at The Palm Press
Production supervision by The Palm Press

Editor: R. Neil Hewison

The author gratefully acknowledges the assistance of Mr Ted Brock and Dr. John Rodenbeck, many of whose invaluable suggestions have been incorporated in the text.
Any remaining inaccuracies are the author's alone.

Cover photograph: A stroll along the river by Luxor Temple
Inside cover photograph: The West Bank and Temple of Hatshepsut from Luxor
Inside back cover photograph: Night falls at Medinet Habu

Dar el Kutub No. 2752/88
ISBN 977 424 189 4

Printed in Egypt by Nubar Printing House

CONTENTS

Introduction

Creation

Before the building of the Aswan dams, heavy rains in the mountains of Ethiopia would bring floods to Egypt. When rainfall in Africa was sparse, drought parched the length of the Nile valley. Egypt, a smear of green in the desert, remained utterly dependent each year on the vagaries of a monsoon far to the south. Since prehistoric times, the Nile has poured from the heart of Africa, occasionally awesome and destructive, but always bearing the promise of new growth, new life.

Changes in the river still affect the lie of the land. In winter, when sluices in the High Dam are shut down and *fellaheen* repair their irrigation channels, here and there, mud banks appear in the Nile. These seasonal islands are soon covered in grass and weeds. On a few, trees take root; on all, birds settle, squabble and devour fish.

In living memory, the Nile flooded each year, in July or thereabouts. Most of what is now dry agricultural land was inundated for several months of the year. And every year the waters receded to reveal islands, which were rapidly over-run with plant and animal life. To the ancient Egyptians, this spontaneous and repeated regeneration must have seemed remarkable.

According to most Egyptian creation myths, life began when land emerged from the waters of primordial chaos. In one, a small mound of mud rises from the flood and on it a hawk and snake appear; they engage in a ferocious battle for mastery of the earth. The hawk gains victory and commands the natural world into being.

This outcome represents the triumph of good over evil, order over anarchy and foretells the ascendancy of the Egyptian state. At the same time, like all myths, the simple story encapsulates a mystery: how is it that human beings came to be on the earth... how did creation itself come about?

Early Egyptians described the puzzle of creation in terms which were familiar to them. They translated the natural forms around them into a complex symbolic language by which they might communicate with the power underpinning the universe. They considered the bounty of the earth to be a miracle sustained only by the continual intervention of spiritual agencies.

Viewing the copious representations of plants and animals which cover the relics of their civilization, we become aware of the vital importance these people attached to the natural world. Living as we do in a civilization which has lost touch with the earth, we are perhaps too ready to judge their thinking idolatrous and jejune. Yet the western cultural heritage has such deep roots in the beliefs of the ancient Egyptians that it would be presumptuous to dismiss their ideas without understanding them.

This guidebook therefore combines a tour of the main monuments of Thebes and selected tombs in the necropolis with a brief historical outline and some basic background information about society and religion in ancient Egypt.

The hawk and the serpent shown on a first dynasty stela from the royal necropolis at Abydos; both creatures became important symbols of royal power

Outline of Egyptian History

Ancient Egypt was the earliest fully-fledged nation state in the world. It became and remained the most advanced technologically and administratively for thousands of years. In a sense, Egyptian history belongs to us all: it is a cornerstone of our own culture.

It was not by accident that high civilization developed in the Nile valley: the environment was entirely appropriate. In the beginning, long term climatic trends had their effect. Around 10,000–8000 BC, what is now the Sahara desert was rolling savannah. As the glaciers of the last ice age receded, rain became scarce and the land parched. From the 6th millennium BC hunter-gatherers of the region, finding even their deepest wells drying up, drifted north and west to the coast, south to the margins of the jungle or east to the Nile valley. Here they joined pastoralists who had filtered down the Nile from central Africa and, finding a temperate climate and fertile land regularly replenished by Nile silt, settled and farmed. Communities grew and prospered.

From the outset, the people of Egypt were a mixture of several African races. Moreover, trade contacts with the East led to cross-fertilization with the emerging cultures of Mesopotamia. The arts and crafts of civilization and particularly the knowledge of writing developed in Egypt and in the city states of Mesopotamia at about the same time, but in Egypt they found the richer soil and quieter times which allowed for sustained growth.

From many parts of the world there is evidence of societies (such as those of bronze-age Britain) which developed mathematics and astronomy to a rather advanced level, but in most cases these early proto-civilizations died out: there is a limit to the ability of a society to transmit and develop its culture without a means of permanent record for its law, religion or commerce. Historians generally date the history proper of a particular culture from the

The Pyramids of Giza - the most enduring monuments of history

time when written records began to be kept. In Egypt around 3200 BC we are therefore looking at the beginnings of the recorded history of the planet.

In Egypt, life was regular and orderly. The Nile valley was isolated by desert barriers to the east and west, and the Mediterranean sea to the north; at that early date, no sudden mass incursions were possible. People went about their daily agricultural round in relative peace. The Nile provided a perpetual source of water and fertilising silt, so, if there was peace, there was usually plenty of food. On the whole, the country was easy to control: the river provided a natural and convenient highway which linked the main centres of population; the people were compliant and for the most part content with their routine.

The unprecedented and unrivalled monuments of the Nile valley could never have been achieved without a high degree of social organisation extending over a large area. This was achieved early in Egypt through enlightened self-interest.

In late prehistory, an understanding developed between communities scattered along the Nile that their common survival depended on one shared resource: the river. Cooperation between settlements in trapping and distributing water resulted in abundant crops.

Between harvest and inundation, there was enough spare man-power available to allow economic organisation and division of labour on a considerable scale. This in turn brought into being leisured political and religious classes and a solid social structure that closely resembled the monuments which Egyptians now had the resources to erect in homage to their god-king.

Some time before the turn of the third millennium, as written records appeared, two major states came into being: Upper Egypt (the valley) and Lower Egypt (the delta). Around 3100 BC, King Narmer united the two by force of arms.

The first king of the first dynasty, usually known as Mena (and who some identify with Narmer), moved the capital of the united state, logically, to the juncture of the two lands, at Memphis, a few miles south-west of modern Cairo. **The Old Kingdom** (2600 - 2130 BC), reckoned from the beginning of the fourth dynasty, lasted some 500 years, with the peak of absolute pharaonic power reached around 2550BC, when the most enduring monuments of civilization took shape: the pyramids of Khufu (or Cheops), Khephren and Menkauré at Giza.

However, the system was not without its checks and balances. There is evidence of political tensions between the priesthood of Re – the official sun god – and the court. The pharaoh claimed to be a god in his own right; the priests referred to him as 'son of Re', thus rendering his claim more conditional.

The pharaoh was, in theory, monarch of all Egypt, but rulers of the *nomes* – or governorates – champed at the bit when-

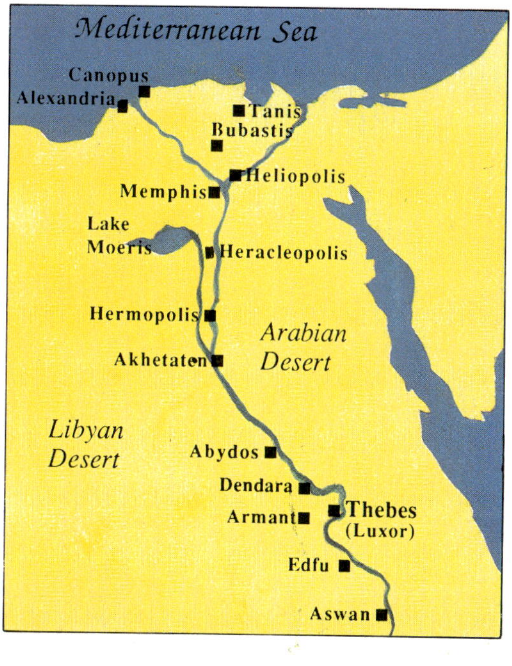

ever the rein of power was slackened. These two factors, together with meagre floods, brought about a weakening of central power. The reign of King Pepi II was followed by about a hundred years of disorder known as **The First Intermediate Period**. Egypt split into a number of smaller states. Now Thebes came to prominence.

Following a long war of attrition with the rival house of Akhtoy, seated at Heracleopolis, the Thebans, under Montuhotep II, reunited the two lands. **The Middle Kingdom** (2100 BC - 1700 BC) began with a compromise between the central authority of the state and that of the regions.

A proto-feudal system was established which was, however, undermined by a number of revolts. These were finally quashed by Senusert III (c.1940 BC).

By the end of the Middle Kingdom, Egypt's deserts were no longer the effective barrier they had once been. From the west came Libyans, from Asia, the Hyksos – horse-borne nomads whose spartan discipline spurred them to dominate the valley of the Nile. **The Second Intermediate Period** (1790-1570 BC) lasted for more than 200 years, the Delta being more or less permanently under the sway of foreign kings.

Thebes again provided the resolution that set Egypt back on course. The Theban king Ahmose vowed not only to reunite Egypt, but to pursue the vile foreigner and destroy him. This vow became the theme of **The New Kingdom** (1570-1080 BC), when Egypt flourished as an imperial power. For over 200 years Thebes was the political capital of the empire. The 18th and early 19th dynasties constituted a high point of Egyptian civilization. The new military strategies of massed archers and chariot charges (probably acquired from the Hyksos) was matched in civilian life by a renaissance in artistic techniques stimulated by contact with the Asian client states.

Problems with a proliferating priesthood resurfaced with the return of more orderly life. Things came to a head when Akhenaten sought to re-establish absolute kingly rule and a less compromised form of

EGYPT AND HER NEIGHBOURS

as shown by imperial tradition

sun worship. He met with fierce opposition from the hierarchy, who allied themselves with a faction of the army to restore 'traditional values'. Under the Ramessides this led to increasing militarization of official life, reflected in the monuments of the period.

During the late 19th and 20th dynasties, Egypt again became the target of foreign invasions. This time, immense, continental movements of tribes in Asia caused upheavals in the northern Mediterranean littoral. Expelled and desperate for a new home, the Sea Peoples fought several times for a foothold in Egypt. They were repulsed, but the state was weakened by the effort.

In **The Late Dynastic Period** (1080-332 BC), the priesthood set up its own independent ruling clique in Thebes. Libyan chieftains took advantage of the disorder and established a dynasty. Kushites from the Sudan – so long despised by Egyptian colonisers – ruled their former masters (rather well) for eighty years. Assyrians swept into the Delta and up the valley. Other foreigners, especially Greeks, settled in large numbers. A minor renaissance of native Egyptian culture flickered briefly around 650 BC, during the **Saïte Period**, but the hated Persians came to snuff it out.

Alexander the Great was welcomed in 332 BC as a deliverer from the Asiatic hordes. However, he stopped short of giving back the land to its native rulers. After Alexander's death, his general, Ptolemy Lagus, became the first of a three hundred-year long dynasty of Macedonian pharaohs ruling from a new, thoroughly Greek capital at Alexandria, (while taking care to appear pharaonic along the Nile). Egypt's African heritage gradually became absorbed into the political culture of the classical Mediterranean.

The last major Ptolemy, Queen Cleopatra VII, exerted great efforts to preserve the nation's independence from the rising power of Rome. But Rome saw vast agricultural resources in Egypt, and moved into the country in force to secure them. Egypt became the personal fief of the emperor.

Although the new rulers also observed the forms of the ancient rites, these had become so corrupted and overlaid with obscurity that Egyptians no longer had enough faith in them to resist the onslaught of Christianity. Thus, along with the rest of the nations subject to Rome, Egypt passed into the Byzantine empire and its modern history began.

KING LIST

Monarchs of the 18th Dynasty *(290 years)*

MONARCH	FROM		TO	YEARS
Ahmose *	1575	-	1550	25
Amenhotep I	1550	-	1528	22
Thutmose I	1528	-	1510	18
Thutmose II	1510	-	1490	20
Hatshepsut *	1490	-	1468	22
Thutmose III *	1490	-	1436	54+
Amenhotep II	1436	-	1413	23
Thutmose IV	1413	-	1405	8
Amenhotep III *	1405	-	1367	38
Akhenaten *	1367	-	1350	17
Smenkhare	1350	-	1347	3
Tut-Ankh-Amun	1347	-	1339	8
Ay	1339	-	1335	4
Horemheb *	1335	-	1308	27

** Major characters*
+20 under the tutelage of Hatshepsut

Principal Monarchs of the 19th Dynasty *(c. 125 years)*

MONARCH	FROM		TO	YEARS
Ramesses I	1309	-	1308	2
Seti I *	1308	-	1291	18
Ramesses II*	1290	-	1224	66
Merenptah *	1224	-	1214	10
Seti II	1214	-	1208	6

Brief History of Luxor

The town we know as Luxor was called الاقصر *al-uqsur*, by the Arabs. It means 'the palaces'. Before the Arab conquest, the ancient world knew the city by the Greek name *θibæ*, the anglicised version of which is Thebes (not to be confused with the Grecian Thebes in Boeotia). The ancient Egyptians called their religious capital *Wâset*.

Until the foundation of the Middle Kingdom in the twenty-first century BC, Wâset was a mud-brick village on the east bank of the river. Of all the settlements in the fourth nome, it was the least significant, paying homage now to the princelings of Hieraconpolis, near Edfu, now to the chieftains of Armant, the local capital.

Around 2000 BC the Armantines took Wâset, an early conquest on their road to the domination of Egypt. Among them Inyotef, who founded the 11th dynasty, was the first to build a tomb of consequence in Luxor.

After the fragmentation of the First Intermediate Period, Egypt was reunited by a grandson of Inyotef, Montuhotep, who fought three generations of northern princes during his reign of fifty years. His efforts brought about the reunion of Egypt and its cultural revival. He was buried in a tomb in the cliff near Deir El Bahary.

The patron deity of Armant was Montu, a warrior god with the head of a hawk. But during the Middle Kingdom the cult of the humanoid Amun gained favour. Although originally a minor god of Wâset only, he was promoted with the victory of the Armantines over the whole of Egypt. In remarkably short order, Amun was amalgamated with the sun god Re as supreme national deity.

The status of Thebes was enhanced as pharaohs began to build costly shrines to Amun. Fashionable royalty and courtiers were buried nearby on the west bank. During the New Kingdom, the city grew in prestige after a native son, Ahmose had repelled the Hyksos. Thebes now became spiritual capital of an Egyptian empire. Under the warlike Thutmosides, tribute poured into the city and trade with her neighbours was on Egypt's terms. The monuments we see today in Luxor come from this era. Houses, workshops, gardens, lakes and palaces spread on both sides of the Nile. Thebes was at its zenith: architecture, the arts, mathematics and medicine flourished in the greatest city the world had ever known.

This city was dominated by its priesthood, which grew ever more powerful. The heresy of Akhenaten dealt a severe blow to the hierarchy, however, and hence their city. This king closed the foundations of Amun and built a new capital near modern Amarna. The old cult was restored with help from the military, and Thebes regained something of its former glory .

But with the state looking more steadily in the direction of the Mediterranean, circumstances dictated the moving of the capital to the north. Thebes remained a leading religious centre, but lost political importance. In the Third Intermediate Period, Theban rulers made a bid for national power, but it was short-lived. The city was sacked by the Assyrians in 671 BC. After the foundation of Alexandria, the decline of Thebes was inevitable.

The city had no strategic value, so it was virtually overlooked by the Arabs, who invaded Egypt in 639 AD. It slipped into rural quietude; its monuments sank into the silt.

This preserved it nicely for archaeologists, who rediscovered Thebes during Napoleon's expedition to Egypt at the end of the 18th century. Many relics of of the city have been looted over the centuries; most domestic buildings, made from mud brick, have vanished. But the Egyptians built stoutly in stone for the god-kings, so the temples and tombs of Luxor remain an enduring witness to their industry.

Court of Amenhotep III at Luxor Temple

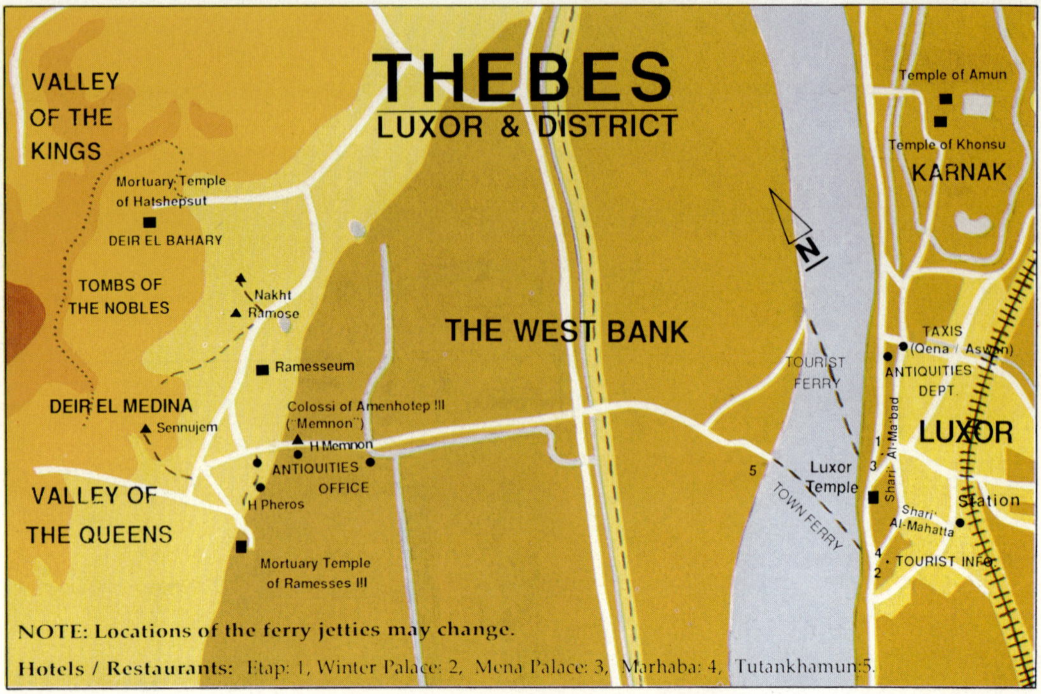

The Town

Modern Luxor presents a jarring contrast to the grandeur of the temples. Noisy, ramshackle, gay, trashy... the streets bustle with life, and you will be mercilessly hustled by all those who live off the tourist trade, from hansom-cab drivers to the handsome youths in galabeyyas who offer distinctly unofficial guiding services to all and sundry. These latter are best declined by those susceptible to silly romantic notions about the Orient.

Hotels. There are a number of cheap and cheerful hotels near the station in Shari' El Talafiziûn. There is a youth hostel in Shari' El Ma'bad. More expensive, but air-conditioned, are the Windsor and the Mena Palace. Higher priced establishments require an exchange receipt to show the origin of your money, or payment in hard currency. A full list of accommodation is available at the tourist office (see map). On the West Bank, the Memnon, Marsam and Medinet Habu hotels are basic but good fun. Less spartan is the Pheros, behind the Antiquities Office.

Restaurants are available for all budgets. Fresh and nourishing local fare can be got cheaply in Shari' El Mahatta and in Shari' El Ma'bad. Fancier, although offering a limited menu, is the Marhaba, above the tourist information office. The terrace has a good view of the river. Unpretentious, european-style cooking can be found at the Mena Palace.

On the West Bank, the Tut Ankh Amun provides a range of modestly priced dishes served *alfresco*. The restaurant stays open late.The luxury package hotels offer the usual overprepared 'international cuisine' for a price. Afternoon tea on the Savoy terrace has its own shady charm, and the tea is good, too.

How to Get About

(see map, opposite)

Donkeys are for hire on the West Bank. Ask at the West Bank jetty of the 'town' ferry. Horses may be had, but not cheaply.

A bicycle is the ideal way to get about Luxor. Bikes can be hired on either side of the river from c.LE3 per day. They travel on the ferry free of charge. Some proprietors require your passport or a deposit. Check the brakes, chain and tires thoroughly before riding away. Insist on a clean machine.

Taxis are far more expensive than in Cairo or Alexandria. Rates vary strictly according to supply, demand and your ability to pay. Don't judge Luxor by its taxi cabbies or by its *hantoor* drivers (the hantoor is a horse-drawn cab also known as a *calèche*). Exercise caution, too, with the felucca (sailing boat) boys, who have studied more tourists' net worth than you've had hot dinners.

Visiting monuments on the East Bank. Luxor Temple is in the middle of town, so there is no need for transport. A *calèche* to Karnak makes an attractive drive along the river. Negotiate a price (LE3-5) before you step inside. Tickets for both temples may be bought near the gate. You are free to wander round the ruins at Karnak from dawn until dusk. At night, the site is roped off for sound and light performances which come in various languages on different nights. Check with your hotel.

Luxor Temple is open in the evening. If you come in summer, night time is a cooler time to visit the temple: the flood-lights display what is left of the ruin to eerie effect and there are fewer people about.

Luxor Museum, on the Corniche, should be visited for its well-ordered display of Theban statuary and other artefacts. It is the right size for a museum; about an hour should suffice to get a clear picture of the materials available and styles current in the New Kingdom. A catalogue is on sale.

Visiting monuments on the West Bank. Cross to the West Bank by the town or tourist ferries. Short stay visitors should expect to part with 25 piastres; residents pay less. Tickets for the monuments are available from an office at the West Bank jetty or at the *tafteesh* (Antiquities Inspectorate). For the *tafteesh*, take a *tax bil nafar* (box taxi, shared with ten others) for 15-25 piastres to the second crossroads west. Student and special tickets and permissions are available only from this office. This is a good point to start your tour of the Ramesseum, the colossi and the temples at Medinet Habu, all within walking distance in winter. Taxis may be hired at the ferry by the hour or day. Prices are seasonal and negotiable.

It is best to visit the West Bank early, taking in the Colossi, the Ramesseum and the Tombs of the Nobles on the first day, then visiting the Valley of the Kings, Deir El Bahary and Medinet Habu the following morning.

Crossing to the West Bank on the town ferry

Photography. If you intend to photograph the monuments, dawn and late afternoon provide the best lighting conditions for heavily atmospheric shots (and there are fewer tourist coaches at that time). However, some reliefs benefit from the contrast afforded by the sun at noon. Outdoor still photography is unrestricted. The use of flash in the tombs is absolutely forbidden. A special permit from the Antiquities Office may be obtained for natural-light photography. Video recording, too, requires a permit. Most varieties of colour film are available, but it is wise to check the date of manufacture. Developing is best done at home.

Dress and Demeanour. In Egypt, especially in the south, dress codes differ markedly from those prevailing in Europe or the Americas. Shorts, worn by either sex, are considered either ridiculous or unseemly. Women who bare their arms invite more attention than they would perhaps wish; hairy arms and legs are considered barbaric and unclean by Egyptians of both sexes.

On the whole, a compromise of light cotton trousers and a long-sleeved shirt is suggested for men and a skirt and blouse with adequate sleeves for women. The hemline should always be below the knee. A light shawl or broad-brimmed hat will help you blend into the background and preserve you from that fried red skin which spoils too many visitors' holidays. Foreign women who have lived in Egypt for any length of time usually find that avoiding the eyes of young men may serve to keep the wolves at bay.

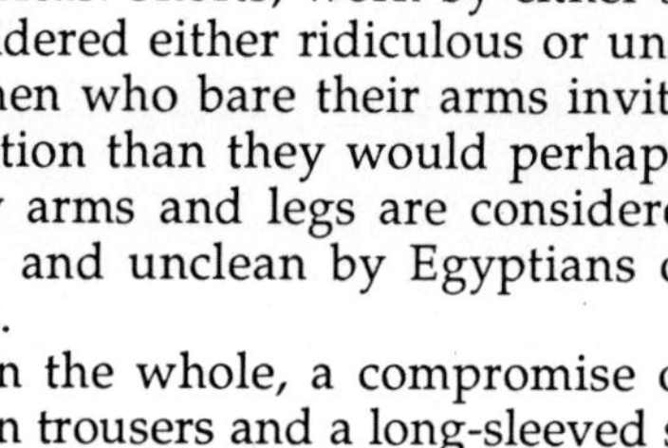

If you come in winter, bring or buy winter clothes; it gets chilly at night, even in Egypt. You will need a sweater or jacket. Attractive, inexpensive clothes can be bought in most Cairo stores. Good quality sunglasses are recommended in all seasons.

Being either over-polite or indecisive in speech puts you at a disadvantage. Being ill-mannered invites worse abuse by return. Don't wander aimlessly about: it always attracts trouble.

There will inevitably be hundreds of attempts to sell you souvenirs or dubious services. Refuse what you don't want. Be polite, but firm. If you see something you like, the best advice is get to know the market price; don't buy first time.

If you must engage the services of an unofficial guide fix the price beforehand in front of an appropriate witness such as the reception clerk at your hotel. Tip people for services that you have accepted – that's how they live.

Advice. • It is sensible to drink only bottled water if you are here for a short stay. Inexpensive local brands are sold, chilled, all over town.

• Should you venture off the beaten track, avoid splashing about in canals. Bilharzia parasites lurk in slow moving or stagnant water. They are painful and difficult to get out of your liver.

• Don't linger in the Theban hills after dark: it's easy to fall off.

• If you want to visit all the monuments without exhausting yourself, your best maxim is early to bed and early to rise.

• If you have not yet done so, register your passport at the Passport Office *(see map)* or make sure that the hotel does this for you. A substantial fine and delay at the airport await those who ignore this requirement.

Rural Thebes

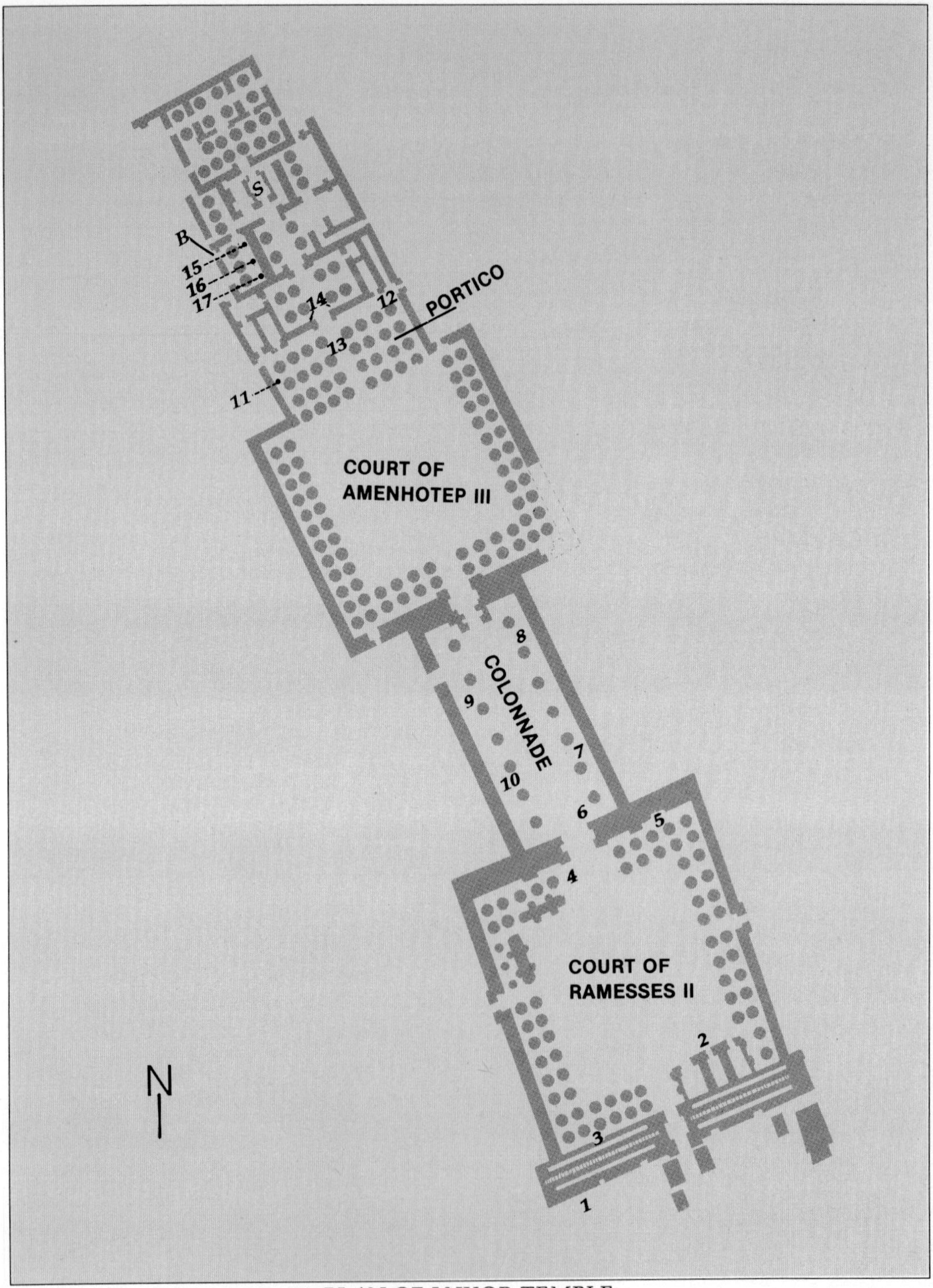

PLAN OF LUXOR TEMPLE

The pylon of Ramesses the Great before the temple at Luxor

Luxor Temple

In ancient Egypt, the temple was the mansion of a living god. The incomprehensible and mysterious power of creation, embodied in the god, was worshipped with elaborate ritual behind massive stone walls.

At the same time, the temple was the seat of spiritual authority. The god's wishes were communicated to the world by a priesthood whose position naturally gave them great influence in affairs of state.

Social order, too, was thought to derive from the ineluctable power of the supreme being. However, access to this power was restricted and strictly hierarchical. Temples were not like mosques or churches: ordinary people were not allowed into these buildings to pray for this or that. Nevertheless, all those with position or privilege to protect strove to magnify the deity. The king in particular would stress his special relationship to the force within the walls. Pharaoh was both the son of god and god in his own right. At the same time, he was the legitimate representative on earth of the spiritual powers and protector of the pantheon.

The temple at Luxor was dedicated to Amun, patron of the Theban nobility who grew, with their influence to be the official state god of Egypt, taking on the powers and responsibilities of earlier solar and fertility deities.

Egyptian temples were usually the home of a subsidiary god and goddess, associated with the principal in a triad. The triad can be thought of as a kind of holy family: there is usually the god, his consort and a son. At Luxor, Amun's 'wife' was Mut, hieroglyphically depicted as a vulturess, otherwise in human form with a vulture headband, and the 'son' was Khonsu, a god associated with the moon.

To emphasise the sacred nature of the god's house, temples were constructed so that the most important parts were the most hidden from the public gaze (much as in traditional Arab domestic architecture). To those human eyes permitted to glimpse him, the god would have appeared as a small gilded statue dressed in expensive clothing, his face carefully made up with rouge and eye-liner. He stood in a naos or shrine at the heart of the temple. Occasionally, Amun would be paraded in the open air. But still he would be veiled, shrouded in mystery, *haram.*

The temple is rightly approached from the north, between two rows of sphinxes with the heads of Nectanebo II. This striking avenue led from the temple of Luxor to the Karnak complex some two miles to the north. More may be seen just south of Karnak *(see map, p.10).*

Pylon of Ramesses II

A pylon announces the temple proper. Formidable, this structure was designed to impress. In its day, it would have been whitewashed and painted in bright colours: reflecting in the glare of the sun, what a stunning sight this must have been! In each tower of the pylon, notice tall, oblong grooves. They were for giant flagpoles from which flew standards of the protective deities of Egypt – long, pointed streamers which had symbolised a supernatural presence from prehistoric times.

The pylon was how the temple showed itself to the world. Those who might care to enter must first acknowledge the might of the pharaoh, here shown as battle-blooded victor. Damaged reliefs on both towers give a somewhat overblown account of Ramesses II's triumph over the Hittites – a people from Anatolia with imperial ambitions. At *1*, in the upper *register* (Egyptologese for 'row') we see scenes from the battle of Kadesh (just north-east of the Beka'a valley in the Levant). Ramesses charges into battle, trampling the wretched Asiatics under foot. At the far left, a Hittite prince flees in his chariot, fearing the wrath of the king of the greatest empire the world had known. More of Kadesh can be seen at Karnak and at the Ramesseum. A less partial assessment of the god-king's battle-prowess appears on page 79.

Before the pylon, statues of the great leader (two of which are seated) add to the impression of untrammelled power. Note how they all seem to be exact copies of an ideal model. They imply that the calm, self-confident pharaoh reproduces himself effortlessly. Of course, it wasn't effortless at all. Ramesses II's monuments demanded mass-production techniques; schools of craftsmen must have laboured incessantly to turn out the thousands of enormous statues and other artefacts created for this mightiest of monarchs.

Were he not a god-king, one might be forgiven for accusing Ramesses II of hubris. In common with many of his predecessors, this pharaoh claimed, in the name of Amun, to have erected rather more than historical fact will allow. While there is no doubt that he raised this obelisk in front of the pylon, his claim, inscribed at its base, to have built the whole temple is absurd, as we shall see.

Obelisks were cult objects originating in the Old Kingdom. They represented rays of the sun. This one, of pink granite, had a pyramid-shaped top covered with a gold and silver alloy (electrum), to scatter the sun's rays. Baboons round the base screech at the rising sun *(see photograph page 15).*

This obelisk had a twin, whisked away, like so many of its fellows, to a European capital as a memento of an earlier empire. In this case, Louis-Philippe of France had the grace to offer a gift in return. Fifteen years after the obelisk was removed, he presented Muhammad 'Ali

Pasha (1805-1848), with a tasteless gingerbread clock which may be viewed in the forecourt of the Muhammad 'Ali Mosque in the Citadel at Cairo.

The obelisk now stands in the Place de la Concorde. When it was pulled down for shipping, a name was found engraved beneath the base: Ramesses II.

Court of Ramesses II

As we move inside the temple, we move back in time. Most major religious foundations were built on the site of an earlier shrine. Buildings which had stood there for centuries were either demolished to make way for a mightier edifice or incorporated into the later structure. As the dynasties rolled by, pharaohs vied with their ancestors in monumental extravagance.

Thus the Ramesses II court, erected around 1290 BC, incorporates three small shrines (at 2), which predate it by 200 years. The shrines, to the Theban triad, were built in granite by the female pharaoh Hatshepsut and revised under her successor and arch-enemy Thutmose III. Ramesses II completed the work and, typically, added his own commentary claiming the shrines for himself.

In a classically forceful attitude, the king strides forward with his left foot (from the first court at Luxor Temple)

The architrave above the entrance of the central room shows a double image of the monarch running to the enthroned Amun. The representation on the left shows the king wearing the bobble-topped mitre-crown of Upper Egypt; that on the right has him wearing the high-backed crown of the Delta. At each end, Amun embraces his son.

Far up to the left of the court, a mosque has sprouted on the mound of rubbish and dirt that formerly buried the temple. This eleventh century Fatimid structure is all that remains of a mediæval village which took advantage of the elevation to escape the annual flood.

On the back of the northern tower of the pylon, preparations are under way for one of Luxor's extensive calendar of festivals. It is the feast of Min (a fertility and harvest deity usually shown with a formidable erection). Here, at 3, a mast is being set up outside his shrine and men scramble up the guy ropes to attach the standard of the god. Min was believed to inhabit this mast, which would enable him to take part in the festivities.

In between the columns of the south and east colonnades, stand statues of Ramesses II, with a somewhat menacing air of self-assured formality; and to each side of the entrance are more representations of the great leader in blue-black granite. Here, the king stresses the unity of Upper and Lower Egypt by wearing a combined crown. The lady to his right at 4 is Nefertari, officially known as the Great Royal Wife.

Most wall reliefs here lack their original colouring and are now badly damaged. They depict Ramesses making offerings and sacrifices to several deities, in the presence of his numerous progeny.

At *5*, there is a small relief showing the temple in the thirteenth century BC. This is an unusual subject for a temple wall and the artisans seem to have had some difficulty in adopting a point of view which would show everything as the eye might see it and yet respect the rules governing religious representations. The pylons, with standards fluttering, are depicted from the front. However, there was a long standing convention that human beings should be done in profile, so the statues of the pharaoh are shown from the side. The traditional representation was thought to contain something of the spirit of its subject; where a king was concerned, it would have been especially unwise to innovate merely for the sake of realism.

Colonnade of Amenhotep III

Move south from the court into the colonnade and the fifteenth century BC. You are now in the main body of the temple, begun under Amenhotep III. This 18th dynasty king, known as "the Magnificent", ruled during a settled period of prosperity. Wealth and artistic sophistication combined to raise and adorn monuments befitting Thebes at the height of its power.

Ramesses II enthroned before the pylon of Luxor Temple

At *6* there is a diad or double statue; it shows most of Amun (who here bears a remarkable resemblance to King Tut-Ankh-Amun) and a mutilated Mut. An equally damaged diad opposite is dwarfed by another enormous Ramesses II.

The colonnade comprises seven pairs of sandstone columns with capitals in the form of open papyrus plants. They would have been lavishly decorated with bright paints, in the bold colours which the ancient Egyptians learned to make from metal ores. When the temple was in use, the impression would have been of a riot of vegetation.

However, the work was unfinished when Amenhotep died and it was left to his descendants to complete the decoration. But his son, Akhenaten, was an iconoclast of the first order; the only work he commissioned here seems to have been the fanatical erasure of all references to Amun and other traditional deities. It was under Tut-Ankh-Amun *(c. 1355 BC)* and later kings that the side walls were added and decorated with reliefs.

Along both walls a series of tableaux show detailed scenes from the main festival of the religious year: the Opet, or wedding anniversary of Amun and Mut.

Amun's principal shrine was at Karnak. The temple at Luxor, although dedicated to the triad as a whole, was also the official residence of the vulture goddess. So it was to this temple, known as the Southern Harem, that Amun Re came on his nuptial visit.

The normal means of transport, for humankind, was the river and naturally, the gods travelled by water too.

At *7*, amid much singing and clapping and shaking of rattles, shaven-headed men in long robes drag the barque of the god to the Nile. Notice the shrine in the middle of the little boat, the standard of the god and the carved heads at prow and stern.

The boat is then towed up river to the temple at Luxor where, in the birth room *(see p. 20),* an amorous rendezvous takes place with the vulturess. Unfortunately reliefs showing this are damaged.

Further south along the wall, bulls are slaughtered and fresh meat prepared for the gods. Acrobats perform and offerings are made at ***8*** to the Theban triad.

The eastern wall (***9*** and to the north) shows Amun's return by boat to Karnak. There are lively scenes of sacrifice, dancing and merrymaking. A number of musicians blow and strum various instruments at ***10***.

The final scene, at the north end of the wall, shows Amun reinstalled in state in his shrine at Karnak *(upper register).*

Court and Portico of Amenhotep III

This court, light and airy *(photograph page 9),* is a masterpiece of uncluttered elegance. It is surrounded by a double row of columns, restrained and decorous, with papyrus buds for capitals; they compare well with the fatter and more florid pillars in the court of Ramesses II. The fluting of these columns refers back to the temples of prehistory, when the roofs of shrines would have been supported by bundles of reeds tied together.

At the southern end of the court four rows of eight columns form a portico (formerly covered). Reliefs show offerings to Amun and other gods. At ***11***, Amenhotep presents calves to Amun.

A number of small and ruined chapels to the triad lead off the portico to the south. At ***12***, there are remains of a stairway which led to the roof of the temple. This was used for an important ceremony at the beginning of the Egyptian year, when the image of the god, normally kept in a darkened chamber, would be exposed to the sun for revitalization.

At ***13*** a Roman altar, with a dedication in Latin to the emperor Constantine, prepares us for the classical anachronism of the following chambers.

Vestibules

As we move further into the temple, the original plan gets rather confused by later additions. One would expect to advance from the portico into the vestibule, where offerings would be brought for the god. But this area was converted by Roman imperialists into a state shrine. The columns were removed and the original relief work plastered over. The entrance to the sanctuaries was transformed into a votive niche where incense would be burned for the emperor and to the Roman pantheon. (Damaged paintings of a number of Roman senators or emperors may still be seen). On the north wall at ***14*** is part of a New Year procession.

Beyond this, a second antechamber still has its four original columns. Since

The Theban triad: Amun, Mut and Khonsu

this part of the temple was hidden from the sun, the reliefs retain some of their original colouring. Many show Amun and other deities presenting Amenhotep with the *ankh* cross, symbolising eternal life.

Sanctuary of the Sacred Boat

The structure we see today (*S*) was originally a third vestibule in which a wooden sanctuary stood. However it was converted into a limestone shrine in the reign of Alexander the Great, who captured Egypt for the Macedonians in 332 BC.

Although he stayed here for less than a year before marching off to his death in Asia, this greatest of Greek generals left his mark all over Egypt. He is shown here on the outer walls of the shrine making offerings of feathers and vases of fine ointments to the triad. Although kings and emperors tinkered incessantly with the temple, its fundamental purpose and ritual remained unchanged. So, inside this holy place, Alexander is shown making offerings to the same gods in the same way as his predecessors did two thousand years before he came. The form of the sanctuary is also quite traditional; it is in effect a chamber within a chamber, stressing the hermetic inviolability of its occupant.

The shrine would have been in darkness most of the time, the little god waiting for his servants to perform the ceremonies. At an appointed hour, a muttering would announce that the high priest had come to cense Amun, anoint his exquisite body and apply cosmetics in the dawn ritual. The bolt is drawn; the heavy wooden door swung open. Then the veil of the naos is lifted and the day begins.

Now the Master Of All That Is is dressed and presented with food and drink from his extensive temple estates. Fish and fowl, fruit and grain; the god is offered copious quantities of every good thing. There can never be enough. Whatever can be brought here is a mere taste of the teeming life which he, Amun, has created.

The words, growing fervent, echo in the half light and mingle with the odours of incense and offerings. And, magically, the prayers of the priest and the smell of the sacrifice are enough to sustain the spirit of the god in his gilded cage .

At intervals throughout the day, sacrifices are brought to the precious statue accompanied by long recitals of liturgy.

At dusk, the final rites accomplished, Amun, all-powerful god of the sun, will be undressed with the delicacy his state deserves and, after painfully elaborate bowing and scraping from the high priest, he will be be put to bed, left to illuminate his stuffy chamber for another long night.

Around the sanctuary, a number of small rooms acted as stores for temple regalia and treasure belonging to the god. Reliefs depict the contents of each room.

In the chamber known as the **Birth Room** (at *B*), Amun and Mut consummated their annual love tryst, thus re-empowering the pharaoh as the son of god. Mut would greet her lord in the guise of Mutem Wia, mother of Amenhotep III. Reliefs here show a goddess holding an *unkh* to the nostrils of the honoured lady (*15*), with the ram-headed potter-god, Khnum, in attendance.

Two little Amenhoteps are shown on the potter's wheel at *16*. Thoth, Ibis-headed messenger of the gods, here acting as a kind of angel Gabriel, announces the forthcoming birth to the lady in the upper register at *17*, and the creator acknowledges his son at the northern end of the wall.

It was considered vital for the maintenance of the natural order that the king's title be beyond question. Thus piety conspired with pragmatism to achieve social and cosmic harmony.

Children take joy rides on the festival boats during the Moulid of Abu Al-Haggâg.

Behind the Shrine of Alexander, a little hypostyle hall or vestibule leads to the original holy of holies, built by Amenhotep III but now destroyed.

Today, the Temple of Amun stands shamefully denuded of its pomp, exposed to the common gaze, stripped of its glory. Its spirit has long since been sucked into the lenses of a million cameras. But, as we return through the broken columns, past the crumbling pictures of the barques of Amun and Mut and the long forgotten Opet festival, the little mosque of Abu Al-Haggâg, perched on the colonnade of Ramesses II's court, reminds us that some still consider this holy ground.

It is before this mosque, in the Muslim month of Sha'ban that the faithful celebrate the *moulid* of Abu Al-Haggâg; at once the birthday and the funeral of a saint whose origins are wrapped in mystery.

On the eve of the full moon, just after noon prayers, a local band strikes up. The whole town turns out to watch, clapping and swaying in time to the music. Christian women sing a funeral song to the saint's spirit (for the powers of Abu Al-Haggâg are recognised by all of God's people).

The chief sheikh, wearing festive robes and turban, moves down the steps from the mosque and, at his signal, elaborately decorated camels rise to their feet to lead the procession, carrying mock coffins of the saint and his consort.

Among the crowd, men and youths from the guild of ferry-men begin their traditional duty: dragging three sacred boats in procession around the temple. It is hard work in the mid-day sun, but they perform with good humour a task which the boatmen, their ancestors, have undertaken for millennia.

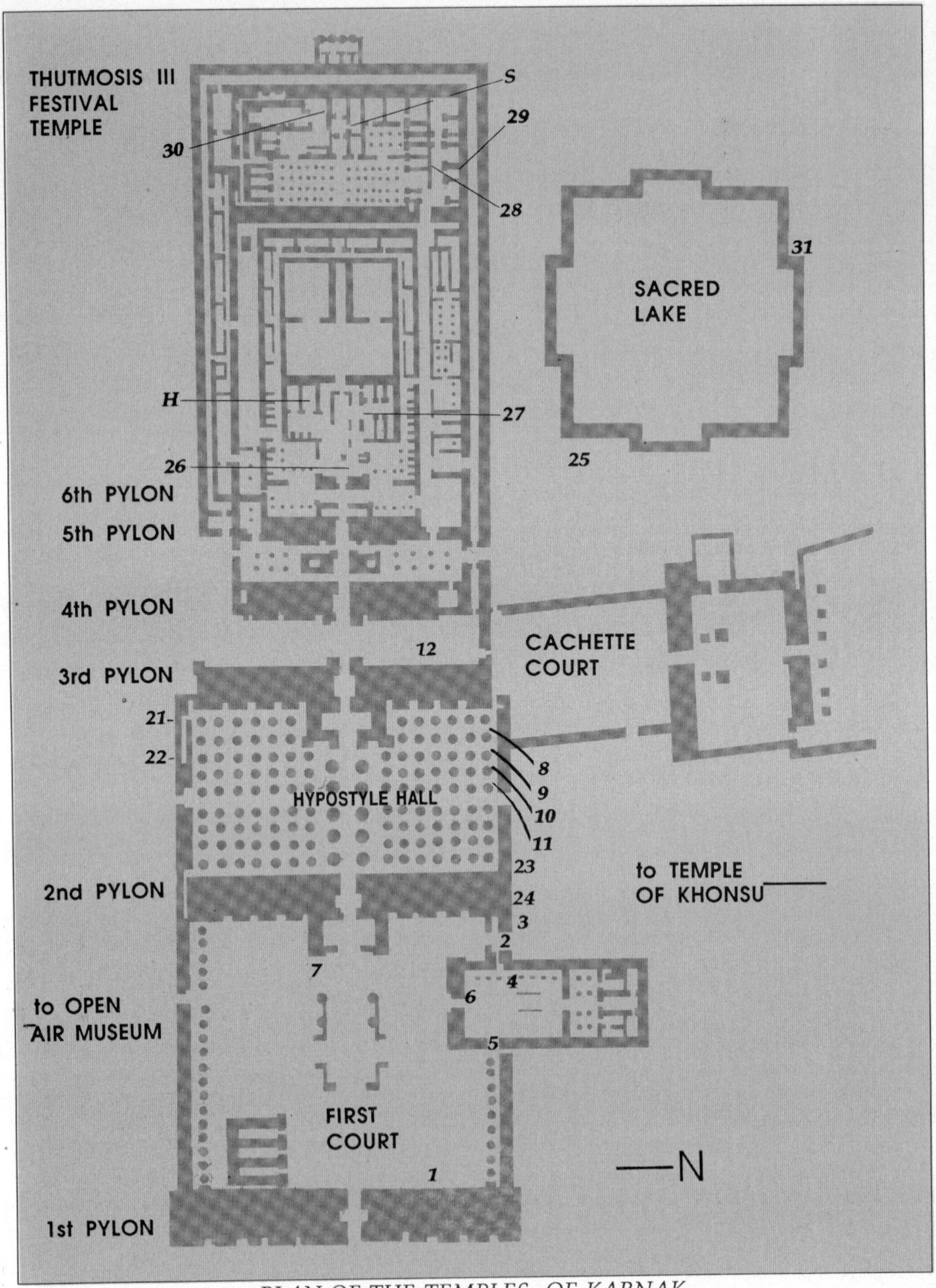

PLAN OF THE TEMPLES OF KARNAK

Karnak just after sunset

The Temples at Karnak

In visiting Karnak, we pay our respects to the most eminent religious foundation of antiquity. Here the Creator was worshipped for over two thousand years – more than the entire span of our present era.

At the heart of Karnak is the Great Temple of Amun. Nearby are smaller teples to Khonsu and Mut, and to an earlier Theban war deity, Montu the hawk-headed. There are several shrines dedicated to gods from other religious centres (such as Ptah of Memphis). Over the centuries, pharaohs commanded monuments to celebrate their victories and jubilees; standing, toppled or buried are innumerable gateways, obelisks and stelæ recording the rise of Egypt and its fall between 1800 BC and the advent of Christianity.

Roman reliefs vie for space with Ptolemaic inscriptions. Pylons and pillars of seventh century kings from Kush (modern Sudan) stand side by side with Middle Kingdom kiosks. But the main and the finest part of the temple of Amun was erected in the age of Egyptian empire, in the New Kingdom, during the 18th and early 19th dynasties *(see plan, opposite).* Under the circumstances, there is a remarkable unity of style. We can note degenerations and quirks in the architecture of Karnak but the basic ideas and techniques remained the same throughout its history.

In the time of Thutmose III, the temple proper began at the fourth pylon. At that time the Nile, or a canal, flowed up to a quay by what is now the first court. But in time the course of the river changed and for a millennium the temple was extended westwards. Many pharaohs were unable to finish what they had started. Some threw up courts and halls in haste, which collapsed almost as quickly, only to be incorporated into later structures. Much, however remains: a unique record of religious and political developments over an enormous timespan.

Shrines to various deities indicate the gods' ranking at different periods. We can discern the economic resources available to each pharaoh. Karnak also gives a clear picture of the cultural environment at the time of construction. In addition, there are graphic records of military campaigns, copies of edicts and treaties, and stelae commemorating public events.

Known as *The Most Select of Places,* Karnak served as a religious capital but also as a centre of intellectual excellence; an unrivalled university of the ancient world. Priests developed a practical grasp of proportion, mathematics, surveying and astronomy together with basic techniques of chemistry and metallurgy. Under their tutelage, the conventions of writing and representation were refined. Sacred drama, literature and the graphic arts flourished and there was a music school attached to the temple. Some orders grew into specialised legal or medical colleges and one class of priests served the community as interpreters of dreams (the psychiatrists of antiquity).

The priesthood was organised under the direction of a High Priest, appointed by the King, although in practice the position was usually hereditary. He was known as the First Prophet of Amun. There were other ranks of prophets below him. The permanent hierarchy was assisted by large numbers of lay priests who forsook their daily lives for three months each year to do their stint in the temple. Men would join an order appropriate to their secular occupation, so lawyers would become priests of Mât, goddess of truth, while scribes would owe allegiance to Thoth, patron of writing.

A priest was expected to refrain from all sexual activities, eat prescribed foods, shave his head and body daily and dip himself in the sacred lake at regular intervals. This régime was to fit him spiritually for his essential role as *Servant of God* - the traditional name for a priest. His main purpose in the temple was to serve Amun through the performance of appropriate rituals. It was only occasionally in the history of Karnak that priestesses were permitted to hold office, but Chantresses of Amun took a supporting role as a singing and dancing team during processions and on certain high occasions.

Associated with the temple were estates of the most fertile land. By the late New Kingdom, the Temple of Amun controlled a quarter of the arable land of Egypt. Virtually all the farms and buildings of Thebes belonged to the plumed god, together with their workers. The staff of the temple itself included cooks, butchers, brewers, bakers, builders, sculptors, painters, craftsmen, cleaners and innumerable serfs and slaves of every degree.

The state religion was so thoroughly integrated into society and the hierarchy at Karnak controlled such vast economic resources, it was inevitable that the priesthood should seek to exploit its power politically. Karnak was pre-eminent in the ancient world as a centre of religious thought and practical science but it was also a hotbed of ambition and intrigue, at the centre of disputes about property and succession and engaged in a perpetual game of push and pull with the pharaoh over who should best interpret the inscrutable mind of the hidden god, Amun.

It is possible here to give only an impression of the great span of history, and merely to hint at the abstruse religious ideas which confront us on the walls of Karnak. It would take the dedicated visitor weeks to see everything of interest. Here we will tour the main temples, mentioning briefly those parts closed for excavation or reconstruction.

Ram-headed sphinx before the first pylon at Karnak

Tour of the Temple of Amun

The approach to the temple is from the west, along an avenue lined with ram-headed sphinxes *(photograph p. 25)*. They are at once rams, sacred to Amun and symbolic of the creative aspect of the solar god, and lions, representing his wrath when roused.

Between the sphinxes' paws are statuettes of the pharaoh. Today these kinglets bear the name of Ramesses II, but they were probably commissioned by Amenhotep III.

The avenue originally extended up to the fourth pylon. In front of the sphinxes, archaeologists found roots of hibiscus shrubs, together with narrow irrigation channels. The garden has now been replanted as it was in antiquity.

Such inspired restoration cannot conceal that the first pylon and first court were built in a period of decline. They were the work of kings of foreign extraction in the Second Intermediate Period, and the execution was often routine. But as we walk east, we rise back in time to the prime of Egyptian civilisation and remains of the New Kingdom structures of Thutmose III and Hatshepsut.

First Pylon

(25th - 30th dynasties : c. 750 - 340 BC)

This pylon was never completed. The vast uninscribed faces of the towers bear bleak witness to the abandoned ambition of Kush. It was begun under Taharqa, a pharaoh from the northern Sudan.

Kush was an Egyptian colony for much of its history, but as pharaonic civilisation wore out, these dark princes came to carry the baton. By then, Egypt was fragmented and in terminal decline as an independent power. Economic collapse prevented the pylon from ever being completed.

The northern tower is about 90ft. high, the south exceeding it by about 12ft. Each is about 170ft. broad.

A ticket inspector waits between the two towers.

Displaced sphinxes wait in disarray in the first court at Karnak

First Court

(20th - 25th dynasties : c. 1200-650 BC)

Impressive as it is, this court contains little of real merit and a lot of imitation. Structures built for foreigners predominate and much of the decoration is merely imitative. Even those buildings erected by kings of Egyptian lineage betray a degeneration of style from that of the New Kingdom. Foreign incursions and shortage of resources brought about cultural decline.

The court is in a mess. Much of the masonry has fallen down, yet parts of it seem to be still under construction. Lines of displaced sphinxes lead nowhere *(photograph page 26).*

At *1*, a pile of black shale covers what's left of mud-brick ramps used in the erection of the 25th dynasty pylon. Another Kushite monument is the **Kiosk of Taharqa**, of which ten pillars and a few fragments of wall remain in the middle of the court. The kiosk would probably have served the Sudanese king as a reviewing stand during important ceremonies.

The Court Walls

(22nd dynasty : c.950 BC)

These walls were thrown up in the Third Intermediate Period, when chieftains of Libyan stock gained at least the red crown of Lower Egypt. They ruled from Bubastis in the Delta. Perhaps the most interesting aspect of their work here is the Gateway or **Bubastite Portal** at 2 and the inscriptions on the side of the pylon at 3 which commemorate the havoc wrought by Sheshonk I in Palestine.

Although there is here no specific mention of a raid into Israelite territory, (which is odd considering the pharaonic penchant for taxonomy), this king is generally identified with the biblical Shishak who grabbed the golden shields of Solomon from the temple of Jehova in Jerusalem *(see I Kings xiv, 25-26 and 2 Chronicles xii, 2-3).*

In the north-west of the first court at *4*, there is the ruined **Shrine of Seti II** *(19th dynasty : c.1210 BC)* in honour of the Theban triad. It would have been used as a resting place for the barques of the triad during festival processions. The shrine is divided into three cubicles. That of Mut is nearest the wall, Amun's in the middle.

The inside walls bear reliefs showing the triad's barques, each bearing a godhead at prow and stern. The decoration inside is rather rough and heavy. It is immediately obvious that the standards of artistic execution, which began to slip with the reproduction mania of Ramesses II, fell even further under straitened circumstances. Seti II reigned for less than six years; this is the only monument of consequence above ground that has been attributed to him.

The Temple of Ramesses III

(20th dynasty : c.1170 BC)

Built standing alone, outside the main temple walls and in its day surrounded by no court, this temple was constructed quickly by pharaonic standards, in under a decade. Work started in the eleventh year of the king's reign.

Ramesses III was a preoccupied man. He had to bear the brunt of serious attempts to colonise Egypt by waves of northerners invading from the Mediterranean. The swagger of his famous namesake's monuments must have accused him everywhere for, unlike his great ancestor, the young king ruled an Egypt in crisis.

His situation was unenviable: he would have felt obliged to do something impressive in stone, but having limited resources, his coffers depleted by war with desperate refugees who provided no booty, he had to cut his coat according to his cloth.

The first known instance of tomb workmen going on strike for their wages dates from his time.

Osiride columns in the court of the temple of Ramesses III at Karnak

This modest temple, dedicated to Amun, has nothing unusual or impressive about it. It was only later in his reign that Ramesses III felt secure and rich enough to undertake a monument commensurate with his achievement, at Medinet Habu.

The pylon is entirely conventional, unlike that at Luxor. Here we see a traditional scene (damaged), known from the first dynasty. The king grasps his enemies by their top-knots and raises his mace to crack their heads open. He offers these wretches as a human sacrifice to Amun, who grants him vanquished cities.

The same scene appears on each half of the pylon, but the king wears the crown of Upper Egypt on the eastern tower and that of Lower Egypt on the western.

Two not-quite-colossal statues of the king put the left leg forward in a conventional attitude of virility. Today, the temple is a miserable affair, almost totally lacking in colour, and the reliefs are far cruder than their counterparts at Medinet Habu. Plaster was used to trick things out, and it smeared somewhat. Now it has crumbled, leaving a slapdash effect.

Later, the walls were much damaged by salt left by floods. But no following monarch interfered substantially with this temple, which makes it unique at Karnak.

Beyond the pylon, a court is flanked by two colonnades with sixteen statues of Osiris at the front of each pillar. The court leads to a portico with just four columns, a vestibule and three gloomy shrines.

Reliefs at *5* show the king followed by a procession of priests carrying the sacred barques of Amun, Mut and Khonsu. These are followed by a procession of standard bearers. Each standard is a glyph symbolising a nome or district of Egypt. At this period, there were forty-two nomes. Some of these standards are seen on predynastic pottery from about 4500BC ; they are older than writing and made a significant contribution to its development. The procession shown here took place during the king's jubilee festival in which, every few years, he demonstrated to the community his fitness to rule the whole land. At *6*, on the inside of the pylon, the king receives the sign for jubilee from Amun.

Returning to the first court, notice at *7* a striking **Statue of Ramesses II** with a daughter, Bant Anta, between his legs *(photograph opposite).* When turbulent priests usurped the throne around 1000 BC and founded their own dynasty, Pennejem, First Prophet of Amun and now pharaoh, tampered with the inscription and inserted his own style and title. The features and stance are typical of the mighty monumentalist; the new name deceives nobody. What Ramesses II did to the sphinxes of Amenhotep, Pennejem did to the statue of Ramesses.

Both suffered a worse indignity; with Pennejem disgraced, the stolen colossus was buried face down in the foundations of the second pylon for three thousand years.

Resurrected, the statue of Bant Anta stands nearly two and a half meters tall.

Bant Anta and Ramesses II before the second pylon at Karnak

The Second Pylon

(18th dynasty : c.1320 BC)

This was erected by the pharaoh Horemheb around 1320 BC. Horemheb was a military man who took advantage of a confused succession and a resulting power vacuum at the end of the 18th dynasty.

The far-flung and profitable empire of Thutmose III and Thutmose IV had culminated in the pomp and circumstance of Amenhotep III: but his son, Akhenaten, *(see pages 6, 57 & 59)* laid down the burden of empire to engage in a mortal power struggle with the priests of Amun, which led to his closing their places of worship and erasing the name of Amun wherever he could find it. He built new-order temples here at Karnak to the sun disk and decorated them in what seems a more naturalistic style.

Horemheb rose to be Chief of Police and Commander of the Armed Forces under Akhenaten. However, on that reviled heretic's death, this ambitious officer, whose duty it was to know which way the wind was blowing, switched sides. Piously promoting his candidacy for supreme office, he tried to out-Amun the hierarchy at Karnak. He played priestly politics *con brio* and within four years, the commander became pharaoh.

Horemheb filled the second pylon with thousands of stone blocks from Akhenaten's dismantled sun temples – the shortest-lived monuments in Egypt's history. The re-use of these blocks served a triple function: first, they made convenient filling for the pylon; second, the outrageous stones had to be hidden somewhere; and third, the inscriptions, being so recently dedicated to a solar deity, could not be sullied with a burial beyond the gates. All in all, a neat solution to an awkward heresy; and eminently Egyptian.

The face of the pylon is decorated with scenes of sacrifice and offerings to Amun and associated gods and goddesses. These formal pictograms were copied from the earlier pylon of Amenhotep III. The workmanship is severely classical, betraying nothing of the oddity and looseness of style that had developed under Akhenaten. Horemheb was perhaps concerned to stress the continuity of his regime with those of his illustrious forbears, through a tightening up of artistic criteria.

Before the pylon is a ruined vestibule *(photograph opposite)*, the sides of which were decorated by Ramesses II and in Ptolemaic times.

Hypostyle Hall

(19th dynasty : c.1300 BC)

One and a half acres packed with thick stone columns over sixty feet tall daze the aesthetic sense. On first encountering such a *tour de force,* what other reaction is possible but that demanded by the power which raised them: awe at the pharaoh whose command could move mountains.

And yet, when our critical faculties return, it is tempting to carp (with the safety of several thousand years between us and their perpetrator) at the vulgar striving for effect which characterises pharaonic macro-art at its most boastful.

This petrified forest has its roots in the idea of the temple as a microcosm of the world. Out of the primæval waters of the Nun emerged the first island; on this island, creation took place. The sky, the air, the dew, the plants and animals, all, in their turn, took form here at the beginning of time. This ideal world is shown in the typical decorations of a temple hall – a midnight sky with stars and astral beings on the ceilings, a riot of vegetation and animal life (quick or dead) on the walls and a thick growth of columns topped with papyrus or lotus buds.

So an Egyptian temple is a tribute to the newly created world and the mysterious force which brought it about. It is also a demonstration of the skill and ingenuity

Remains of a vestibule before the second pylon at Karnak

of its craftsmen and the material resources of the pharaoh. In time the grandiloquence outpaced the devotion; the living god grew proud of his works, and the colossal became *de rigueur.*

This hall, the largest of any temple in the world, was commissioned three thousand years ago by Seti I. He was the father of Ramesses II, who completed the decoration here, and the effective founder of the 19th dynasty. There are 134 columns of which 12, with open lotus capitals form a central nave. Rising to 70 feet, these are taller by the height of a man than the rest; the building was originally roofed and the space between the greater and lesser pillars afforded some natural lighting. Other, smaller apertures in the ceiling would let in a few dramatic fingers of sunlight, which would pick out details of the richly-coloured reliefs. The hypostyle hall was a mysterious mixture of the delicate and the massive, the exuberant and the overwhelming; the light of faith wrap-ped in the gloom of formalism.

During construction, however, this place would have been bright and noisy with the regular chanting of gangs of labourers. Where the visitor now stands was covered with a mountain of mud bricks. The columns were built in sections, then the area between filled in with adobe, so the ground level rose to that of the columns. More segments would be locked in place and more bricks piled round them. Massive sandstone architraves were laid on top of the capitals. Gradually, the infill would be dug away, and craftsmen decorated the columns on the way down. In the end, the hall was cleared of debris, and the columns stood proud.

Each column was inscribed with the names of the king in the royal cartouche (Seti I in the northern half and Ramesses II in the southern). The central part of the column bears a scene of offering to Amun, Khonsu, Mut or other deities associated with Amun. There are also cartouches of later Ramessides. Traces of colour still survive on most of the capitals.

Notice the difference in quality between the work done in the time of Seti I and that of his successor. The northern representations are done in high relief; that is the main part of any god or hieroglyph stands out from the surrounding background. However, the work done for Ramesses II in the south of the hall is in sunken relief. Here, the outline of a feature is carved deep into the stone, and the most prominent part of it lies level with the main background *(see figure, p.33).* Obviously, the work of chiseling away large areas of surrounding column was tedious and time consuming. With the coming-of-age of mass-produced art in a time of martial propaganda, aesthetic or spiritual considerations may have taken second place.

The inside face of the second pylon has gigantic representations of Seti and Ramesses before the Theban triad.

The hypostyle hall at Karnak, looking towards the east

Some good examples of recurring themes may be found on the south wall of the hall as follows. At *8*, in the upper register, Ramesses II is being blessed by Horus, the royal falcon god, and the ibis-headed Thoth. The goddess Nephthys offers him the *ankh* of life. Here, Ramesses is acclaimed as king of the two lands – Upper and Lower Egypt – and wears a combination crown to prove it.

Below, in a scene from the jubilee festival, Thoth, acting as secretary to the gods, inscribes the names of the king on the leaves of the sacred ished tree. The king received a new name for each year of his reign. Ramesses, seated in the tree, receives his divine right from Amun. Mut – known by the vulture-band round her head – and Khonsu look on.

At *9*, *(upper register)* is another part of the ritual of the jubilee festival in which the king runs to Amun with jars of ointment. Below, a vigorous recoronation scene takes place.

A little further west along the wall, at *10*, Thoth and Horus again stress the unity of Egypt by binding together the lotus and papyrus plants of the valley and the delta. In the middle, a pair of lungs with windpipes are the hieroglyphic sign for *unite.*

At *11*, the king offers calves to Amun-Min. Many representations of Amun show him with the attributes of other gods; he thereby absorbs their powers. A favourite combination is with the ithyphallic deity Min from Coptos, just north of Luxor, of whom more later.

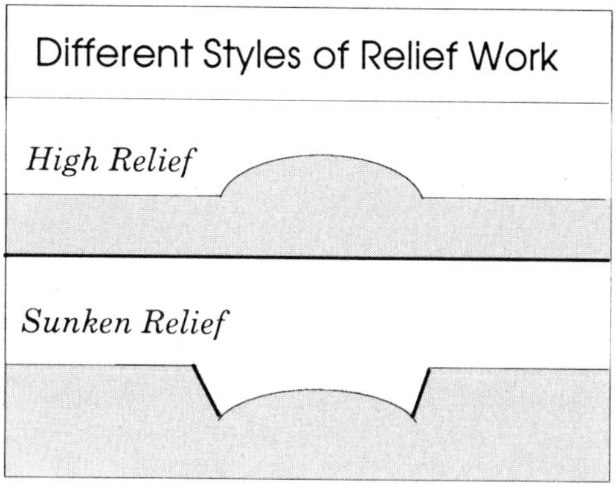

High and sunken relief

Third Pylon

(20th dynasty : c.1370 BC)

Built for Amenhotep III and partially decorated under Amenhotep IV (who later took the name of Akhenaten), this pylon was redecorated by Seti I and Ramesses III when the hypostyle hall was added. The character of the pylon altered when it was incorporated into the temple; it lost its primary defensive character. Some of the original reliefs may be seen in an outdoor museum *(see next page)*. In its new role, the face was decorated in a restrained, traditional manner.

This pylon, too, contained its dark secret. During restoration, blocks were found that dated from the Middle Kingdom. More digging revealed a complete kiosk of Senusert (Sesostris) I in limestone and another of Amenhotep I in alabaster. That of Senusert I is the oldest structure in Karnak, and has been reassembled in the outdoor museum along with other kiosks and pieces of ancient masonry.

Frankly, it is a mystery to Egyptologists why these kiosks should have been put in the pylon. Perhaps it was hoped that this monumental ingestion could fortify the pylon's spiritual effect; perhaps it was the nearest infill to hand. Whatever the reason, we are fortunate in having two interesting structures in excellent condition that would, in the normal course of events, have degenerated into shattered fragments by now.

On the back of the pylon at *12*, there are formal lists of tribute from foreign subjugates brought by Amenhotep to Amun.

Limestone Chapel of Senusert I

The Open Air Museum

(extra ticket needed from the main kiosk)

The visitor with time to spare may, at this stage, care to tour the nearby Open Air Museum. Of particular interest are the three 'chapels' dug from the pylon of Amenhotep III. These chapels probably acted as way-stations or reviewing stands for the Theban triad during jubilee festivals. All three bear scenes of coventional trials of regal strength.

The Red Granite Chapel of Hatshepsut has not been re-erected, since not enough of it was found. In fact, the stones are in such good condition that the chapel may never have been erected at all. However there are many complete panels to be seen on the extant blocks. They were probably carved ready to be assembled.

An advantage of the Red Chapel is that we may see, without craning our necks, excellent representations of important rites and symbols. The style is simple and the workmanship fine. Particularly note at *13*, birds, representing souls, with raised 'hands' and the crest of a plover.

At *14*, the queen, wearing the white crown of Upper Egypt, runs a ritual race with a bull. She is carrying the royal flail of office but no paddle. However, her regal false beard is firmly in place.

On the black granite blocks of the entrance and at the corner, Nile deities bear gifts of abundance. At *15* acrobats perform while a harpist strums. Amun-Min, thinner than usual, appears over 30 times.

The Limestone Chapel of Senusert I (Sesostris I) displays a fugal precision of technique and taste in its decoration that points to an aesthetic pinnacle achieved during that monarch's reign.

The king is shown before the composite Amun-Min. During the Middle Kingdom, there was some rivalry between the supporters of Min and Amun regarding who was the original god of the Armantines. Eventually the usual compromise was reached through amalgamation. On a chapel pillar at *16*, the king, wearing the white crown, steadies the mast of Min, to ensure the fecundity of the soil and underlining his own irresistible potency. At *17* he embraces the god.

This chapel also bears around the base invaluable inscriptions recording the distances between various cities of Egypt and the height of the Nile at these places in various seasons. They are accurate and reveal a formidable surveying ability and the civil service to support it. There is also a standard for ancient Egyptian measures.

The Alabaster Chapel of Amenhotep I is chaste in its decoration but unusually florid in its stone. Reliefs show (on the south wall) jubilee festival scenes, including a fine tableau of the king proving that he remains in good health by running a race with an oar in his right hand. Further to the right, he steadies the mast of Min. A relief at *18* shows the king offering cones of bread, incense and other gifts to Amun.

Elsewhere, at *19*, a few sandstone blocks have survived from the gateway of the third pylon. They show Amenhotep IV about to smash the enemies of civilization into oblivion in the prescribed manner.

Of note at *20* is part of an octagonal column found buried beneath Middle Kingdom ruins of the Temple of Amun. An elongated cartouche contains the name of King Inyotef and the first mention of the name of Amun found at Karnak. Other fragments of various blocks indicate that the craftsmen of Thebes were masters of several techniques, from the delicate scraping-away of alabaster to the more muscular chiselling that granite demanded. In every stone they achieved astounding precision.

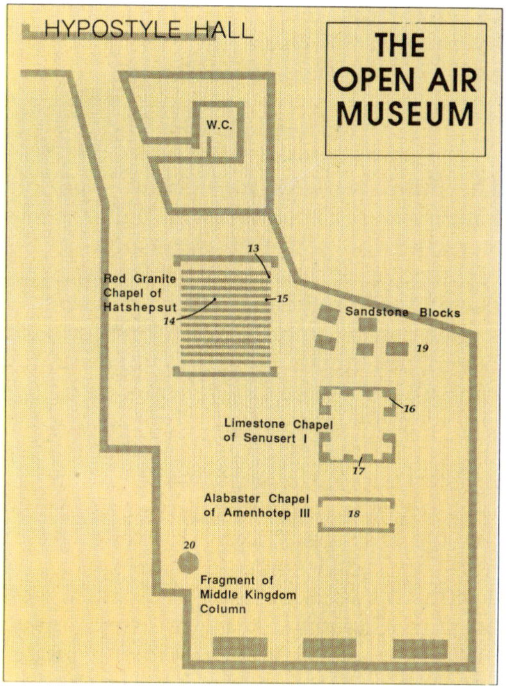

Senusert I salutes Min

To resume your tour of the Temple of Amun, return from the Open Air Museum to the north wall of the hypostyle hall.

Exterior Walls

(20th dynasty : c.1370 BC)

The outer walls of most New Kingdom temples were decorated with battle scenes to record the perdition of enemies of the resident god. Naturally, these also reflected well on the incumbent pharaoh.

Seti I led a number of forays into the Levant, recognising that if Egypt could not control her Asian approaches, someone else would surely have designs on the fertile black land of the Nile. At **21** *(upper register)* and to the west, we see his majesty in triumph carrying captive princes under his arms back to Egypt, followed by lines of Syrian slaves for the service of Amun. Way-stations in the Sinai, together with Canaan (Gaza) are mentioned, and cedar wood is shown being loaded aboard Egyptian craft in the Levant.

At **22**, the victorious troops, laden with chattels, cross water (shown as a vertical band full of snapping crocodiles) into Egypt proper from Sinai and are welcomed by priests. Further west, the loot is offered to Amun.

Thutmose I and Thutmose III as Osiris in the vestibule beyond the third pylon at Karnak

On the southern walls at **23**, we find more battle scenes and stories, this time from the historians of Ramesses II. His coup de theatre at Kadesh figures prominently here. At **24**, just north of the Bubastite Portal, Ramesses II may be seen leading scores of captive Asian cities on strings. The cities appear as cogwheel-like cartouches, with their names written inside. Each bears the head and bound torso of a native prisoner.

Further north there is the actual text of a treaty made between him and the Hittites. Its flowery insistence on peace and brotherhood sits somewhat incongruously next to the usual scenes of vicious slaughter.

The Earlier Temple

(18th dynasty : c.1530-1440 BC)

Passing between the towers of the third pylon, we come to a narrow court, with one 70-foot erect obelisk of Thutmose I and others, fallen. As at Luxor, obelisks were set up before the entrance to the temple. The fourth pylon was the first in the time of the Thutmosides.

Beyond, the temple is in romantic ruin, massive fragments of wall and statuary giving only a vague impression of its former magnificence.

A narrow **Vestibule** *(c.1515 BC)* follows, with 14 truncated columns, built under Thutmose I. The western wall of the vestibule is lined with twenty-two statues of Thutmose III depicted as Osiris, in mummy wrappings. Another pair guards each of the north and south doorways *(see photograph, this page)*. The obelisk to the left – the largest in Egypt at 90 feet – was put here, with its fallen partner, for the pharaoh-queen Hatshepsut, who acted as regent during the first part of the reign of Thutmose III. On her death, Thutmose, who was pursuing something of a vendetta against his powerful relative, encased her obelisks up to the ceiling of the vestibule, so they were effectively invisible. He also dismantled other of her public buildings and erased her name throughout Egypt.

In this case his action preserved the obelisks rather well. The top of the other obelisk may be seen by the sacred lake at 25.

Although this seemingly petty obscuring of monuments and defacing of titles has been interpreted popularly as evidence of an extended family feud, we may note that such alterations of the wall texts had been going on from at least the Middle Kingdom.

It seems the living pharaoh inherited from his predecessors all their works and offered them anew to Amun, their common father. The reattribution of cartouches may therefore be considered a necessary, if time-consuming amendment to the legal record.

A little further into the temple more examples of the 'vendetta' of Thutmose III abound. Particularly, the reliefs in room *H* show clearly that the image of Hatshepsut has been systematically destroyed. Otherwise, they are in surprisingly good condition.

Fifth and Sixth Pylons

In ruins, these pylons were built by Thutmose I and III respectively. They were both decorated with bellicose scenes, most of which have now crumbled, together with lists of conquered enemies who are shown as torsos springing from fortress cartouches *(photograph opposite)*.

The **Hall of Records**, between the two, was built by Thutmose III. Here, priests inscribed accounts of the tribute accredited to their god.

At 26, two unusual columns of pink granite terminate in stylised carvings of the lotus (west) and papyrus plants, respectively symbols of Upper and Lower Egypt, united by the will of the pharaoh. They seem oddly modern, recalling the turn-of-the-century style of *art nouveau* (which was in fact influenced by a revival of interest in Egyptian techniques).

In moving a few feet east to the **Sanctuary** *(Macedonian: c. 320 BC)* we step forward a thousand years in time. King Philip Arrhidaeus, half-brother of Alexander the Great, himself briefly king of Egypt, replaced an 18th dynasty structure with this crystalline granite shrine. Remarkably, considering the unstable conditions at that period, the decoration here is of a high standard.

At 27, the king receives blessings from Thoth and Horus, and the ram-prowed boat of Amun and that of his consort are carried by priests.

A graphic pharaonic convention shows the status of this Nubian tribe

Festival Temple of Thutmose III

East of the sanctuary, the Temple of Amun degenerates into stumps and boulders. Here, foundations of Middle Kingdom structures are all that remain. But, crossing to the far side, we find a relatively well preserved 18th dynasty structure. This temple, possibly built to mark a major jubilee festival of the king, is set at right angles to the temple of Amun.

The **Hypostyle Hall** comprises fifty-two pillars, thirty-two of them square, but with the central row of twenty having capitals in the form of inverted cups. Some commentators have fancied they resemble tent poles. The design is top-heavy and was never repeated. The hall is surrounded by many rooms and chapels, now in ruins.

As briefly mentioned above, a jubilee festival was performed at irregular intervals throughout a king's reign in order to prove him fit to rule and reinvigorate him if necessary. The ceremony involved trials of strength such as running round a course and shooting arrows. Having demonstrated his prowess, the king would be reconfirmed in office by the gods and his names inscribed on the leaves of a sacred tree.

Seth teaches Thutmose III to shoot (from a corridor in the Festival Temple)

The origins of these rituals are lost in prehistory (although similar ceremonies are still held today in parts of central Africa). There is some evidence that, in predynastic times, the king was put to death if he could not complete the course. The king's magical power to keep chaos at bay and guarantee a good harvest was thought to disappear if he died a natural death. In earlier times, he may have been killed if he weakened and his powers passed to his successor.

Although, at the height of New Kingdom civilisation, Thutmose III would have nothing to fear if he stumbled, the ancient rites were retained.

On the corridor wall at *28*, Thutmose is shown running with vases and oars. Nearby is a damaged relief which depicts Seth and Horus teaching the king to shoot .

The rooms behind the corridor, mostly in poor condition, are connected with the king's central role as a guarantor of the land's fertility. At *29*, Thutmose may be seen embracing the priapic Min, indicating he partakes of his generative power.

At *30*, a small, ruined **Hall** with four lotiform columns is decorated with reliefs of animals and plants (many of them fanciful) which were brought by Thutmose III from the Levant during his campaigns.

There may have been a ritual requirement for the pharaoh to bring back to the temple – that model of the original island of creation – all species of fauna and flora not known in Egypt. By now, Amun was god of all lands, not merely the state of Egypt.

The **Shrine** at *S* was restored under Alexander the Great. Reliefs inside show him adoring Amun and presenting traditional offerings.

Southern Buildings

The buildings and monuments we have visited constitute less than a fifth of the area within the main enclosure (built by Thutmose III). There are also smaller enclosures for the temples of Montu and Mut, currently closed to visitors.

Return to the area just east of the third pylon. Walk southwards through the gateway (of Ramesses IX) and you will find yourself in the **Cachette Court.** Erected by Thutmose III, the walls were decorated by Ramesses II and bear the text of the latter's treaty with the Hittite king Metwallis. There is also a long list of the victories of Merenptah *(1224-1214 BC).*

Early in this century, a shaft was uncovered here containing a *cachette* of thousands of statues, ritual tools and vessels. These had been buried by priests not because the material was valuable in itself, or the workmanship especially fine, but probably to protect the statues and hence the souls of their human originals from desecration in an uncertain future.

The **Seventh Pylon** was raised by Thutmose III and shows the king in the traditional pose, clubbing enemies for Amun. The doorway is of granite, formerly with an alabaster lintel. The area beyond the eighth pylon is currently closed to visitors while a team of French archaeologists restores the Temple of Mut.

To the east of the First Court is the restored **Sacred Lake**, which measures 600 by 360 feet. It was connected by underground channels to the Nile. Here, priests would bathe to achieve ritual purity. There is also a nilometer which provided vital information regarding the annual flood.

The lake had symbolic as well as practical functions. In particular, it was a representation of the original ocean of chaos, the Nun, out of which all was created. In this connection, sacred dramas were enacted on the lake confirming the triumph of the sun god over the powers of darkness in a ritual hunt.

The lake was also home to a flock of geese – sacred to Amun – which were let in each morning through the gate at **31**.

The sacred lake at Karnak

The Temple of Khonsu

A visit to this temple, which lies in the south-west of the main enclosure, is worthwhile, except for those with a strict timetable to maintain. It is in quite good repair and refreshingly complete compared with most of the larger structures.

Khonsu, it will be recalled, is the third member of the Theban triad and a god of the moon. He is usually depicted as a child, with his head shaven except for a patch to one side which is grown in a long lock curling down to his shoulder. This is how male children wore their hair in ancient Egypt. Nothing else distinguishes him from an adult in a typical representation *(see pp. 19 & 57.)* Over his head, Khonsu wears a horned moon with the disk of the full moon in it.

Like the Temple of Amun, that of Khonsu was built over many years, and we meet the later parts first. A large ceremonial gate introduces the temple. It was part of the **Propylon**, offset slightly from the main axis of the building, and constructed by Ptolemy III *(c. 240 BC)* who is shown offering to Khonsu, Isis and Osiris at ***1***. Rectangular pillars fronted by sphinxes lead to the temple. Only a few remain.

These pillars formed a colonnade which led to the **Pylon**, built in the 21st dynasty *(1080-950 BC)* and decorated with scenes of the First Prophet, Pennejem, making offerings to Khonsu, Mut and Amun. The scenes are extraordinary, in that they represent the High Priest as pharaoh – a daring usurpation of the sacred function of the king. Although monarch and priest were each essential to the proper functioning of the Egyptian scheme of things, their roles were always quite separate. The king was an incarnation of the timeless principal of kingship, the priest merely temporal servant of the god.

By the tenth century BC, however, the person of the pharaoh was no longer such an awesome figure. While several dynasties ruled from the northern Delta, most of Upper Egypt was under the sway of Thebes. At this time, Amun had become less specifically a sun god, more of a su-

PLAN OF THE TEMPLE OF KHONSU

preme being in the modern religious understanding of the term.

Such was the prestige of Amun that, with the state divided and the distant pharaoh of doubtful legitimacy, it was natural for the priests to make the final step and assume temporal power on behalf of their spiritual master.

Cartouches of Pennejem

At this stage, Amun was said to be king of Egypt and the priest his direct representative. Even so, there are many instances where Pennejem does not presume to write his name in the royal cartouche

The **Forecourt** was erected by Herihor (c.1000BC), another priest-king of Thebes. There were originally two rows of four papyrus-bud columns to each side of the court and a portico with a further twelve at the back. Those to the north show Herihor offering flowers and perfume to various gods.

On the inside of the pylon, Pennejem is shown before Khonsu and Montu. In the central register, a representation of the temple recalls an earlier relief at Luxor *(page 18).*

As we move further into the Temple of Khonsu, the ground rises noticeably. This indicates that as we near the god-head, we are elevated from the chaos of the everyday world to the sacred island of creation.

The small **Hypostyle Hall** has just eight columns, raised by Ramesses III and IV. The four middle columns are taller than those at the side, and end in open papyrus plants. Most of the decoration shows later Ramessides. On each side of the door, at **2** and **3**, appear the sacred barges of the boy-god and his kin.

Oddly, Herihor is presented both as High Priest and Pharaoh. On the architrave, a damaged relief shows demiurges representing the elements adoring the moon.

The **Sanctuary**, of an earlier date than the rest of the temple, was possibly built for Amenhotep II *(1540-1425)* however, the cartouches were mostly changed to those of Ramesses IV *(c. 1160)*. There are the remains of four pillars and a complete sandstone altar decorated with a Nile-binding scene. Wall reliefs show offerings being presented to Amun.

Surrounding the sanctuary are a number of store rooms of the Roman period. The squatter figures and unsure reliefs are in clear contrast to the more detailed execution elsewhere in the temple.

A stairway at **4** leads to the roof of the temple, whence a splendid view of the whole of Karnak may be had.

Ramesses IV offers a gift of incense to Re Harakhte in the second court at the Temple of Khonsu

Colossi of Amenhotep III

The West Bank

From the West Bank jetty of the town ferry *(see map, p.10)* the road twists up sharply to the left off the flood-bed of the Nile then runs west through bright green fields of sugar cane to the foot of the *Gurn* – that pink, pyramid-shaped hill at the southern end of the limestone Theban range. As you leave the river behind, the contrast between the domestic industry of the fields and the barrenness of the mountains could not be clearer. You are moving towards the land of the setting sun, the desert and the dead.

The West Bank was more densely populated in ancient times: the town of Thebes spread along both sides of the Nile. But nearer the mountains, mud-brick dwellings gave way to more monumental architecture. It was here that the chieftains of Thebes, and later pharaohs of the New Kingdom, caused to be built massive funerary monuments to assist their passage into the world beyond the west.

Colossi of Amenhotep III

(commonly called the Colossi of Memnon)

Your approach to the necropolis is marked by two enormous statues of Amenhotep III, (who began the main part of the temple at Luxor.) The seated statues are battered, yet have not lost their power to impress. Although this 18th dynasty king was not so determined a monumentalist as the later Ramesses II, it was he who started the trend towards massive statuary. These official portraits are carved from a rose-coloured crystalline sandstone from Gebel el Ahmar, near modern Cairo, and were brought four hundred miles upstream by barge – all sixteen hundred tons of them. They stand over sixty feet high.

On the sides of the king's thrones, Nile gods are shown binding together lotus and papyrus plants – symbols of Upper and Lower Egypt. This favourite theme shows how the pharaoh, in his person, guarantees the unity of the state and, like the Nile, brings prosperity to the land. Carved by the legs of the statue nearer the road, Amenhotep's mother (left) may be seen along with his favourite wife, Tî.

The colossi stood before the first pylon of the mortuary temple of Amenhotep, which, with its associated buildings, stretched a quarter of a mile back towards the mountain and covered an area of nearly three hundred thousand square feet. To the south of the temple stood a palace with extensive gardens and a vast lake. As his reign progressed, the pharaoh would spend more and more of his time here, supervising the details of his funerary arrangements. Both he and the priesthood knew it was essential that the king pass smoothly into the fields of reeds (the Egyptian paradise) for the state to remain in good order. This was the main purpose of a mortuary temple.

But a series of high floods undermined the inadequate foundations of the temple soon after the pharaoh's death and left the whole undertaking in sorry ruin. Meanwhile, Amenhotep's son, Akhenaten was presiding over the humbling of the god of his ancestors and the ruin of his dynasty.

The statues, however, remained and an aura of mystery enveloped them, especially after an earthquake opened up a large crack in the northern figure. This caused it to emit an eerie whistle when the rock heated up or cooled.

A legend grew up that it was inhabited by the spirit of Memnon – a mythical Abyssinian hero of the Trojan wars. He was said to be son of Eos, goddess of the dawn who, inconsolable on hearing of his death, thereafter wept each morning for her son; the dew her tears. Thus the wailing of the statue as the sun rose was Memnon calling to his mother to dry her eyes. The emperor Septimus Severus put a stop to this nonsense by filling in the cracks with cement in AD192.

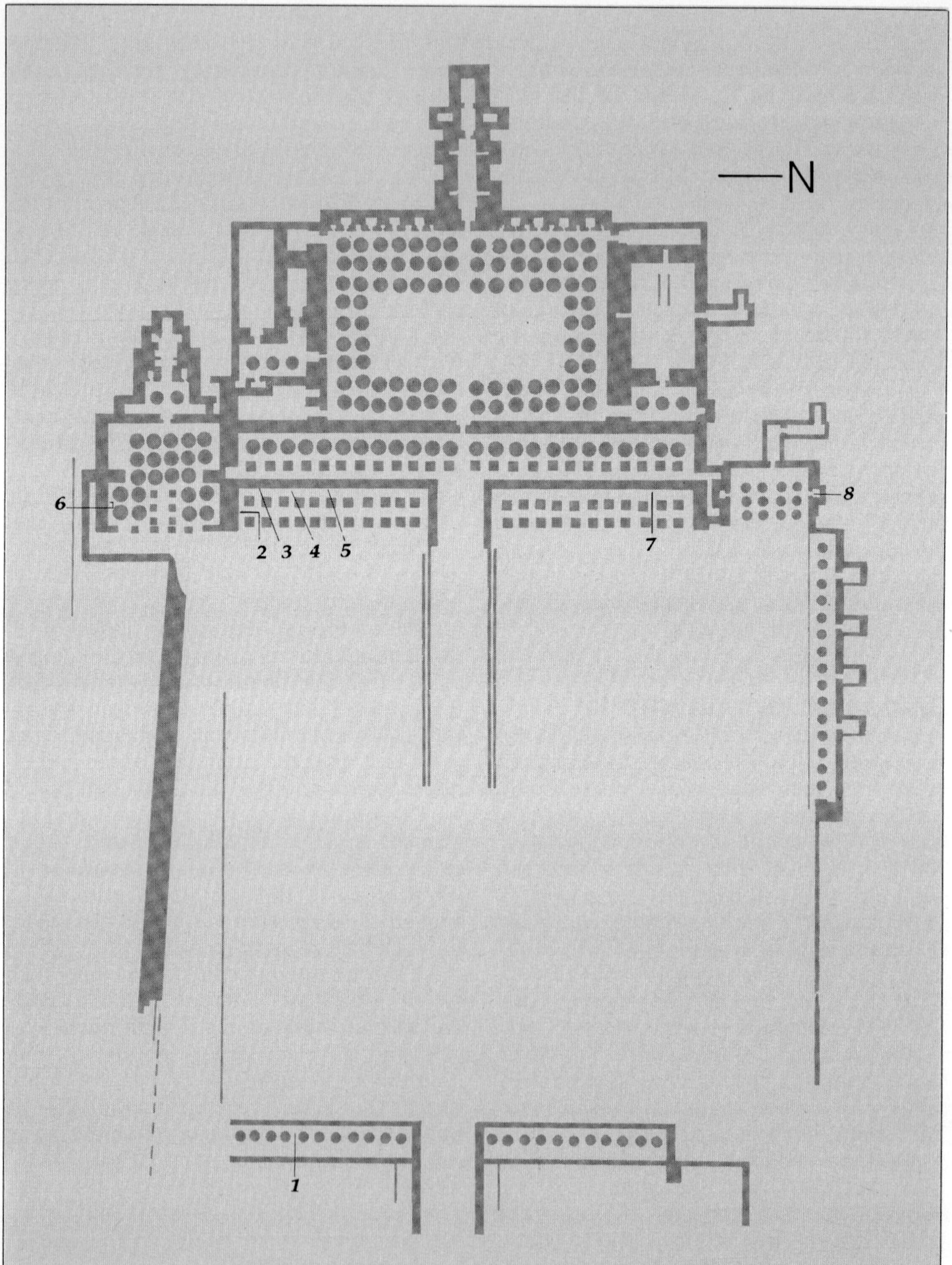

PLAN OF THE MORTUARY TEMPLE OF HATSHEPSUT

Mortuary Temple of Hatshepsut at Deir El Bahary

Although not the first queen to rule Egypt, Hatshepsut was first to refer to herself unconditionally as pharaoh. She put on the kingly false beard and wore the garments of a man without a blush. She was a remarkable woman and a remarkable king. While her sex prevented her from leading Egypt into military engagements, she made up for a lack of prestige in the field by sending a major expedition to Africa and by erecting monuments all over Egypt which still remind us that she was no second rate potentate.

Queen Hatshepsut, daughter of King Thutmose I, became principal consort of Thutmose II, her half-brother. He died prematurely, as did so many of this clannish family, but Hatshepsut exercised great influence in the choice of a successor.

Thutmose III succeeded to the throne while still a boy. Hatshepsut was appointed regent but before long unmasked her ambition and had herself proclaimed pharaoh. It was twenty-two years before Thutmose retrieved his birthright. What better apprenticeship in statecraft could the young king have desired?

The keystone of Hatshepsut's success was her elevated birth: she was daughter of Queen Ahmose, the *Great Royal Wife* (or *God's Wife of Amun*) of Thutmose I, who, however, bore him no sons.

This hereditary position of great royal wife was of no little importance at court. Although the hierarchy of power was firmly in the domain of the male, women – especially those of the royal household – still reserved certain inviolable privileges that had come down to them from prehistory. Royalty was matrilineal (rather as, even today, jewishness is passed down through the mother). To be authentically

Queen Hatshepsut swaddled for the grave

pharaoh, it was deemed that a man should be the son of of a great royal wife or, failing that, should marry her daughter. In the right hands, this requirement became a political tool of considerable potential.

A hieroglyphic text at Karnak recounts how Thutmose III was chosen by Amun to be his father's heir: Amun made a progress in his litter through the temple courts one day in search of a successor to King Thutmose II. He halted before the future monarch, who is described as a mere lad. The youth prostrated himself but the god raised him from the floor then led him before the king and anointed him as the official successor.

Given that the god's word was final and that he was well-advised by his priesthood, it is not impossible that an alliance might be formed between a powerful priest and a determined queen. If Hatshepsut could have persuaded her clerical ally that a particular young man might

An unusually undamaged portrait of Hatshepsut from the second colonnade

find favour with Amun, there were a hundred concupiscent princes of the blood royal waiting to be invited to the great nuptial bed. Of course it is impossible to establish exactly how things happened so long after the event; what we think of as human nature today would perhaps appear perverse in the extreme to an ancient Egyptian.

The Temple of Hatshepsut involved a radical departure from 18th dynasty style. There were no boastful pylons and no gloomy hypostyle halls. The temple was modelled on a much earlier design; that of the mightiest king of the 11th dynasty, Montuhotep, who reunited Upper and Lower Egypt after the disorders of the First Intermediate Period. He was the first to build on any scale in western Thebes; the remains of his mortuary complex may be seen just to the south of Hatshepsut's. Some of the stone was taken for the new temple, which was conceived on a far grander scale.

The building of the 18th dynasty structure was supervised by the Great Steward of Amun, Sennemut, a commoner who became the queen's most trusted advisor and, according to tradition, her lover. It has three terraces, the first two ending in a colonnade of decorated square pillars. On the back wall of each colonnade Hatshepsut recorded major events of her reign. Connecting the terraces is a steep ramp. The third level is a hundred and twenty feet above sea level and right beneath the rock face of the Theban cliffs.

The ramp lies directly opposite the main entrance to the temple of Amun at Karnak. This would facilitate the god's access to the queen's monument during his annual tour of the principal mortuary temples of the West Bank. This happened during the *Festival of the Beautiful Valley*, when Amun visited the temples of the kings, and the citizens of Thebes brought (and consumed) offerings of food and drink for the souls of their buried kin.

The harmony of the temple's design with the fluted cliff, its setting, is undeniable and has often been admired. But unfortunately much of the relief work is severely damaged. When the great lady finally 'went to the west' after a reign of more than twenty years, Thutmose III was determined to expunge all references to her from the architectural record. So most of her cartouches were changed to his and there are many examples of her eyes being scratched out. This went on wherever she had built a monument, but especial effort was exerted in her mortuary temple to make the female pharaoh a non person. Political or legal factors *(see p. 37)* could have demanded a rewriting of history, or the erasures may have been for personal motives: suffering too long in the shadow of the dominant usurper might have poisoned the king's mind against his mentor. In any case it is clear that Thutmose III hoped to pursue his vengeance beyond the

The Temple of Queen Hatshepsut, set against the fluted sandstone Theban cliffs

The Queen of Punt

grave; by attacking the spells engraved for the queen's protection on the walls, he would weaken her resistance to the monsters of the *Dwat*, or underworld. What remains is, however, an invaluable record of an unusual episode in Egyptian history. On the southern wall of the first colonnade at *1*, reliefs show obelisks being floated down the Nile on barges. They seem to be well guarded by a company of archers, and a trumpeter announces the obelisks' arrival at Karnak where they were set up before the fourth pylon. One is shown standing (behind the fifth pillar from the south). Other men carry palm fronds and standards. To the north, Hatshepsut runs the familiar Jubilee race.

The colonnade at the west end of the upper terrace presents a puzzle to geographers of the ancient world. At *2*, Hatshepsut's emissaries are shown bartering goods in a primitive village, where the huts are on stilts. The village is clearly in Africa, but no-one is quite sure where. In the middle register, at *3*, the bearded leader of the native community is pictured, together with a grossly fat negress (perhaps suffering from elephantiasis). They are usually styled the King and Queen of Punt, although both are shown in less state than would be proper for royal personages.

The west colonnade constitutes an account of the expedition to Punt, ordered, we are told, by Amun himself and despatched by Hatshepsut. The main purpose of this expedition was to bring a good supply of incense back to Thebes for use in the worship of Amun.

Punt was for a long time thought to be in the Horn of Africa but more recent scholarly opinion has located it in north-eastern Sudan. Wherever Punt was, it is clear that the queen saw this as an important mission: perhaps it had some magical purpose of which we can be only dimly aware.

The imperial ships are shown preparing to return at *4 (upper and lower registers)* and we can make out among the goods being loaded on board ivory, ebony, leopard-skins, live baboons and gold. Most importantly, there are also tubs containing myrrh trees for production of incense. These were eventually planted here at Deir El Bahary, in the second court, where their roots have been found. In the 18th dynasty, the open areas of the temple would have been shady and cool. At *5*, the queen is shown offering the spoils of her expedition to Amun.

To either side of the colonnade are chapels. That on the left (to the south) was dedicated to Hat-hor, the great mother, a cow-headed goddess representing the sky, and a guardian of the land of the west.

Column-capitals in the shape of Hat-hor

Hat-hor was a complex entity with many responsibilities, whose origins lie in the African stone age. A royal solar deity, often shown bearing a sun-disk between her horns, she was an entirely appropriate choice for Hatshepsut's chapel.

The extant columns are finely carved, their capitals in the form of a human-faced Hat-hor but with the ears of a cow. To the side of each capital a relief shows Horus, the hawk god who signifies legitimate kingship, wearing the two crowns of Egypt and with another token of majesty, the cobra, rearing at his feet.

Hat-hor wears a sistrum or box-rattle on her head. This rattle, which made a metallic twanging noise, was a sacred instrument used in religious ceremonies. It is a symbol of universal harmony – a vital concept for the ancient Egyptians. They understood that all things of this world are in motion and that this motion is underpinned by harmonic principles. Hat-hor, the divine patron of music, was held to harmonise the resonance of events (birth, growth, decay...) and ensure the right movement of the universe through time.

Sokaris receives a gift of wine

Inside the chapel, most images of Hatshepsut have been replaced by those of Thutmose III, but the ritual acts shown are probably copies of the originals.

At *6*, we see the king/queen drinking life-giving milk from the udder of the holy cow. This, it was trusted, would restore vitality to the royal corpse. On the back wall of the chapel, on each side of the door, Hat-hor licks the roused monarch's hand.

The northern wall of the second colonnade (*7*), returns us to the difficult subject of Hatshepsut's title to the throne. Setting an example for Amenhotep III *(see page 21 Luxor Temple)*, Hatshepsut resorts to the expedient of divine coition to legitimate her claim. The annunciation and creation scenes appear in greater detail here than in the birth room at Luxor Temple, but they elaborate the same theme. Defiantly, Hatshepsut has herself described as a boy in the hieroglyphic commentary. At the same time, she does not deny her human parentage; to do so would have detracted from her genetic correctness.

At the northern end of the birth colonnade there is a small chapel dedicated to the jackal Anubis, tutelary of the necropolis. It complements that of Hat-hor; each is dedicated to a guardian of the unknown ways. In a small forecourt there are three rows of chastely carved polygonal columns; reliefs show Hatshepsut (scraped) making offerings to Amun and to deities associated with the world to come. In particular, notice (at *8*) small pots of wine to the hawk-headed Sokaris, who here represents the potential for regeneration after death.

The desert-dweller Anubis was minister to the dead. A vital ceremony for the departed, the *Opening of the Mouth*, took place in his presence. A priest, wearing a jackal mask, would make to prise open the reluctant jaw of the deceased with an adze to enable the breath of new life to enter the body. This process was clearly of great importance; there are many spells in the *Book of the Dead* designed to ensure that the operation would go smoothly. It would also have been performed on statues of the queen, understudies in case her corpse should go missing.

Queen Hatshepsut may have wished to revive the early dynastic custom of being interred beneath her mortuary temple. At the same time, she needed to claim a plot in the Valley of the Kings. Seeking an ingenious combination of the two, she had Sennemut dig eastward from the royal necropolis just over the mountain, planning to locate her burial chamber beneath the temple sanctuary. It was not to be. Rock falls frustrated the neat scheme and she had to be content with a humbler tomb in the valley with the male kings.

At the uppermost level of the temple a colonnade is faced with proud statues of the queen, swaddled as a mummy for death, in the way that Osiris, lord of the underworld, is usually shown. Behind is a court, rooms for various ritual purposes and a shrine to Amun, which was excavated from the face of the cliff. There is a vestibule with a flight of steps at the end leading to the sanctuary. Reliefs in the vestibule show the queen and her daughter making offerings to Amun in the presence of Thutmose I and Ahmose. The innermost chamber with its rather crudely done reliefs is not of the New Kingdom; it dates from Ptolemaic times. By then, not only had Egyptians forgotten how to to draw properly: they had forgotten Hatshepsut.

Hat-hor: goddess of the sky, of harmony and protector of the western ways

One and a half millennia after the great queen's death, her mortuary monument became *El Deir El Bahary* – 'the Northern Monastery.' The temple suffered greatly from monks who chiselled without mercy at the pagan walls.

The teachings of Jesus were embraced nowhere in Christendom with greater popular fervour than here in Egypt. But a strain of joylessness, if not of fanaticism may be detected in those early days when the end of the world was awaited with confidence by every true believer.

Withdrawal from society, at least for a few years, became a social necessity for respectable young men. The nation's deserts were riddled with the caves of eremites and ascetics. The great monuments of their forebears became refuges for meditation on the folly of worldly power and idolatry. The spiritual message of their ancestors had withered through centuries of priestly mumbo-jumbo. Three thousand years after the rise of the Egyptian theocracy, the energy had dissipated into lifeless ritual and was unable to withstand the onslaught of the urgent Christian message.

It is not so surprising that these devout huddles of bored young men should have attacked the hated reminders of a heathen past. Just as Thutmose III hacked out Hatshepsut's eyes and Horemheb obliterated the image of Akhenaten, so these Christians desecrated the old gods' shrines to expunge the error of their ancestors.

It was an ancient Egyptian tradition.

Osiris, Lord of the Netherworld (from the tomb of Horemheb)

The Necropolis

It is to the ancient Egyptians' firm belief in an afterlife that we owe our understanding of their culture. Rock-hewn tombs painted with magical pictures, sandstone temples inscribed with historical accounts and votive colossi carved in granite provide a unique record of life and ideology thousands of years before our time.

The extensive monumental record was intentionally made to last and specifically religious in character. It tells us much more about ancient attitudes than we may learn from the remains of any comparable society of a like date. Without it, very little would be known of Egypt in antiquity.

Naturally, we should not understand all that is shown on the tomb and temple walls in a literal sense. Most of the decoration is symbolic and presents the aspirations of priests and pharaohs: an ideal order of things – the completion and perfection of known physical reality. However, enough incidental detail appears to give us an insight into people's daily lives as well as their leaders' spiritual speculations.

The Egyptians' compulsion to record their ritual activities in stone teaches us virtually all we know of their world. To understand a little about their society, we need to know something of their religion – that essential part of their world view. Unfortunately, the ideas which confront us on the walls are at first sight obscure and often difficult to grasp.

And yet many of their notions lie hidden at the heart our own traditions. Like Jews, the ancient Egyptians maintained strict dietary regulations and imagined a god with a special interest in their own society who could turn vengeful if provoked. Like Christians, Egyptians of the New Kingdom believed in a god who was a man, son of the creator, who died and was reborn as redeemer, judge of the dead and king of the world to come. Like Muslims they believed that the ideal state should be governed by the power of god acting through the ruler according to a strict prescription.

But secreted in the soul of their religion were far older and essentially timeless themes:

The Egyptians perceived in nature and in human nature a life force which surpassed understanding and could not be adequately described in words. The gulf of speculation between what existed, and what could be understood resolved into a number of specific questions: what is the nature of the created world?... how did humankind come to be?... what lies behind the endless cycle of generation, growth, decay and death?

These themes were elaborated by the Egyptians with subtlety and passion from ancestral ideas about fertility and death common throughout black Africa.

Until not so long ago, in most central African societies the king played a vital role in ensuring a successful harvest. He

In the netherworld, the sun-god appears as a ram-headed hawk (tomb of Siptah)

Hatshepsut runs the Jubilee race (from the Red Chapel at Karnak)

was often known as the *rainmaker*. The rainmaker was not necessarily a king in the modern sense, rather a taboo figure, eating special foods and protected from normal human intercourse. The king had to be in sound health and of good physical appearance. If he was injured or grew sick or frail, he was killed. To allow him to die a natural death would unbind his magic from human control, and this threatened disaster to the crops and the tribe.

This ritual murder of the king and the transmission of his protective powers to a chosen successor was considered essential for the survival of these societies. Only in the late nineteenth and early twentieth centuries, under the influence of colonialism and modern nationalism have these practices died out in tribal Africa.

A number of prominent Egyptologists have argued from predynastic evidence and using modern ethnographic techniques that the king was indeed killed in Egypt. The jubilee festivals of historical times, in which the pharaoh was required to demonstrate his prowess and fitness to rule, are thought to be direct descendants of an earlier, and deadly serious test *(see page 38)*.

The transition in which a victim-king became an all-powerful ruler and god in his own right was an intrinsic part of the development of Egypt into a nation state. The king's fertility functions were retained, but the more gruesome sacrificial aspects were dealt with symbolically. The king-who-must-die became a mythical figure – Osiris, while the living pharaoh assumed the warlike and protective features of Osiris' son and heir, Horus. By the beginning of the dynastic period, it was the exercise of military power to protect the state and political power to control society that distinguished the king of the Egyptians from his more innocent and vulnerable forebears.

Osiris was acknowledged throughout Egyptian history as the first legitimate king of Egypt. He is an archetype of the rainmaker. His cult, which has many parallels among other African and Middle Eastern societies, was associated primarily with fertility of the land. Bulls were slaughtered at seed-time and the growth of the corn was connected with his resurrection from the dead. It was only in later periods that he became a personal saviour god concerned with spiritual and ethical values in the modern sense.

On his death, the pharaoh's spirit was said to be united with that of Osiris. The person of the monarch combined the controlling aspect of the solar deity, (whom he represented to his people) with the regenerative elements of the fertility god. His presence was essential for the more important religious rites. The ceremonies surrounding his death remained vital to the welfare of the land and its people (as with those of his predecessor the rainmaker). This is why the passing of the king was attended by such elaborate ceremonial.

Valley of the Kings

As the crow flies, the Valley of the Kings is a quarter of a mile from the temple of Hatshepsut but as the donkey climbs the journey takes about an hour. The views are invigorating but the cliffs precipitous. If you venture over the Theban hills on foot, be sure to go carefully, since the paths are steep and covered in loose shale.

On the other hand, going by bicycle along the tarmac road gives a good idea of the remoteness of this part of the necropolis. It's a steady climb of about half an hour, and the terrain is dry and forbidding. The Arabic term for the area, *Biban El Mulûk* (Gate of the Kings) refers specifically to the straits at the entrance to the valley, guarded during the 18th dynasty. Security was tight since tombs of earlier kings had been stripped of their treasure. It was thought that here, at least, no thief would dare to try his hand.

Here, nothing grows; the valley knows no human seasons, no time of flood and harvest. Far from the Nile in their mountain fastness, generations of god-kings lay in confident expectation of eternal life. The priests' rituals, the magical messages on the tomb walls, the fervent prayers of his subjects all combined to assure the monarch that this was just the beginning.

Meanwhile, slipping barefoot by the guard at dead of night, generations of grave robbers plied their grisly trade, stuffing rough sacks with the carefully arranged funerary goods, rifling through the mummies' bandages for amulets and jewels. The person of the king was inviolable throughout his life, but when he died, his *ka*-soul would know the intimacy of impudent fingers in the dark.

There are few grave goods to see in any of these tombs, and most mummies were long ago removed by priests to the safety of a cache near Deir El Bahary. But what is on the walls is quite startling. We are led, with the king, into the underworld, and see sacred things that no-one was ever meant to see.

It is difficult, now so may people tramp up and down the narrow corridors, to bear in mind how forbidden these places were. Their locations were secret; workers were confined for life to a guarded necropolitan village where they worked, married and died. The spells were for the shade of the king and for the powers at the other side of death; the pollution of the common gaze would spoil them and expose the pharaoh to danger. A right crossing over for the king was central to the maintenance of social order; these things were not to be taken lightly.

The Theban Hills (seen from Medinet Habu)

Tomb of Thutmose III

(No. 34, c. 1450 BC)

Deities protect the king in the anteroom of the tomb of Thutmose III

One of the first tombs to be built here was hidden high up in the folds of a crevasse at the extreme south-west of the valley; you will need good legs to climb up to and down into it.

Thutmose III *(see pages 7 and 38)* was Egypt's first great imperialist; his valour and statesmanship brought immense prestige and wealth to Thebes, but his tomb is modest and chastely decorated. It is nonetheless impressive for its taste and untrammelled dignity. Having climbed to the door of the tomb we now descend an undecorated corridor to the **Well Room**, a sudden pit, bare except for a frieze of bound reeds around the ceiling. Now the well room is fitted with a bridge, but formerly it may have served as a trap for unwary grave robbers and possibly a drain in the unlikely event of rain.

A short corridor, also unadorned, leads to an **Anteroom** in the shape of an irregular rectangle, with two square pillars. The ceiling is covered in five-pointed stars done in gold on a royal blue background, giving a sudden impression of richness. The stars symbolise the limitless eternity to which the pharaoh aspires.

On the walls, black stick figures of many hundreds of deities invoke their protection for the king on his last journey. Although many of these demiurges are obscure and their mandates strictly limited, the king would wish to leave no area of his future unprotected from the forces which could deprive him of his deathright.

To reach the sarcophagus we must now turn sharp left. In the north-west corner of the anteroom a short flight of steps leads down to the **Tomb Chamber**. It is a rectangle with rounded corners. Four small storage rooms lead off the long sides.

This chamber is inscribed with scenes

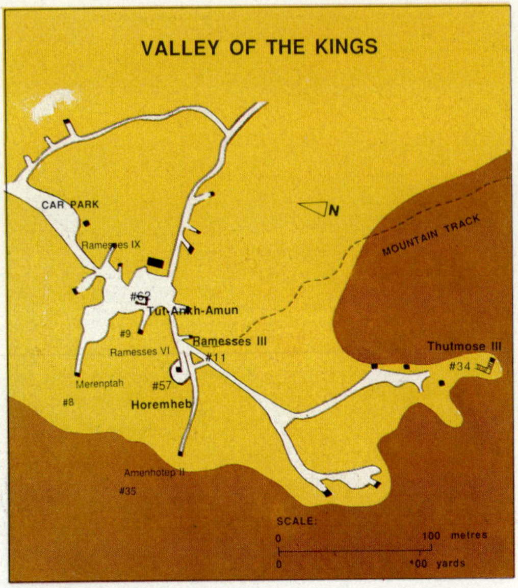

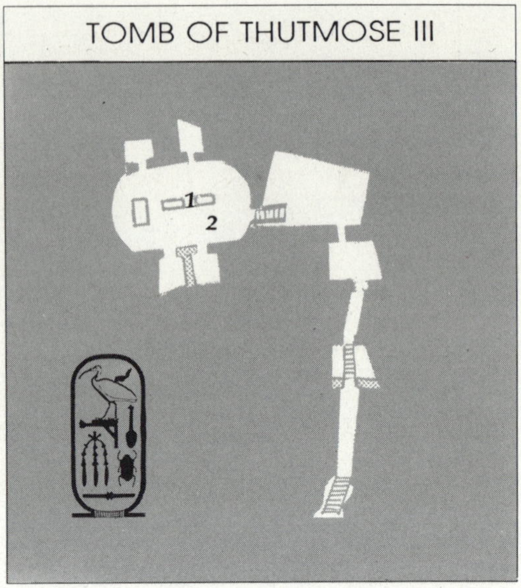

from the pharaoh's private edition of the *Book of the Dead,* (the *Book of What is in the Dwat*)featuring the journey of the sun through the night, and the dead king through the underworld. The pale gold background represents an unrolled papyrus and the figures are done in simple brush-strokes in imitation of the scribes' technique in that medium.

At *1*, on the first pillar, the sun god appears in a number of forms in an account of his nightly journey through the underworld. At *2*, the king's mother may be seen travelling in a boat; below her, some of his wives. Although the early dynastic practice of burying the pharaoh's wives with him had long since been abandoned, the monarch was, at least theoretically, in need of company on his journey.

The mummy of the king is no longer here. During troubled times at the end of the 21st dynasty prudent priests whisked it off in haste to the safety of the Deir El Bahary cache. However, the sarcophagus of red painted quartzite remains on its alabaster pedestal.

Some Egyptologists suggest that the decoration of these early tombs would have been accomplished in the seventy days which elapsed between the death of the king and his burial. During this time, the body would be eviscerated, the vital organs stored in 'canopic' jars, and its cavities filled with natron to dessicate and preserve it. The natron would be removed and the corpse re-stuffed with cloth. Then the ancient morticians would apply cosmetics to the face, and perfumes to cover any lingering odours, and the deceased would be wrapped in his final swaddling.

The store-rooms off the burial chamber would have been filled with funerary goods for the king's use in the afterlife. A few pieces were discovered when the tomb was investigated in 1916. Together with a wooden statue of the king and some alabaster vases, they are now in the Egyptian Museum along with the king's mummy. With a sense of ancestral decency, the late President Sadat suggested that the mummies in the Egyptian Museum, suffering from changes in humidity, be re-interred.

Tomb of Tut-Ankh-Amun

(No. 62, 18th dynasty, c.1350 BC)

Imperial Egypt during the 18th dynasty amassed vast wealth and achieved a sophistication of civilization unprecedented in the ancient world. As with most empires, that of the New Kingdom was conceived in the pursuit of security, grew in greed, and degenerated into lassitude and internal bickering.

A chronic power-struggle between the pharaohs and their priesthood distracted later 18th dynasty monarchs from their military duties. Whereas Thutmose III and IV had sought glory in the field and kept the hierarchy compliant with foreign booty, their successors preferred to magnify themselves in the throne room. Finding the leisure to contemplate their state, they began to believe that the royal house had become compromised by the clergy. Amenhotep III and his son thus sought an opportunity to untrammel their power from the web of scheming priests.

This culminated in an attempt by Akhenaten *(see page 30)* to sweep the old order away. He closed the foundations of Amun and proclaimed a new monotheism centred on the power manifest in the sun, with its cult emblem the *Aten* or sun-disk. Abandoning Thebes for his revisionist capital at Amarna, Akhenaten gave a name ending in *-aten* to many members of the royal family, including his child son-in-law, Tut-Ankh-Aten .

The handsome youth grew up in the heady official optimism of the new city and acknowledging the customized philosophy of his father-in-law. But the envious forces of reaction gnawed secretly from within the palace walls. Both the heretic's vizier, general Horemheb and the boy's tutor, Ay, kept up contact with the priests of Amun and harboured ambitions beyond the title of their blood. On Akhenaten's death, the ten year-old was appointed king in Amarna. But, within six months, Ay had removed the lad to Thebes, renamed him Tut-Ankh-*Amun* and installed him in empty pomp to be ruthlessly manipulated by the powers behind the throne.

The boy-king dressed as the boy-god, Khonsu

The tomb of the little king is small indeed; not that it was built for him. It was probably intended for a state official; a king, however young, would deserve better than this. When the tomb was discovered, it was largely undecorated and showed every sign of having been prepared in haste. Perhaps the death was unexpected. Some speculate that the young man may have been murdered – his skull bears the mark of a possible blow. Certainly Tut-Ankh-Amun lived in unsettled times.

On his death, it is clear that a serious power struggle took place between the royal family and certain parvenus. An extraordinary papyrus letter from the young king's wife (who was now a God's Wife of Amun and thus in a position of some influence) invites the emperor of the Hittites to send a prince to marry her and thus become pharaoh. Other sources indicate that the prince was duly dispatched, only to be murdered on the road by an unknown party. A short war with the Hittites ensued. Meanwhile, the resourceful Ay, with the support of the hierarchy, seized the throne and the 18th dynasty was done for.

The tomb is tiny, but in one respect it remains the most important discovered to date. Although it was robbed in antiquity and resealed with the sign of the jackal – seal of the royal necropolis (*1*), most of the grave goods were intact when the tomb was reopened by Howard Carter in 1922. This gave modern Egyptologists a unique opportunity to study and gloat over the gold coffin and masks, weapons, furniture, jewellery, votive statues, ornaments and domestic objects of an exceptional period. There was even a whisk fitted with ostrich feathers (probably a symbol of royal authority rather than a device for swatting demon flies). Particularly interesting was the golden throne of the boy king which shows him anointed beneath the sun-disk as Tut-Ankh-Aten.

The tomb walls also betray the influence of the Amarna style of art: a certain squatness in the figures and a looseness of line shows that those who inscribed the walls had grown accustomed to a different canon.

The arrangement of the rooms is straightforward. Steps lead down through a plain corridor to an anteroom (*A*) with a store-room (*B*) off. These were packed with supplies – jars of wine and seed – together with a surprising quantity of grave goods. It took Carter and his team ten years to remove and catalogue the hoard.

To the right of the anteroom lies the burial chamber. Originally, this was concealed by a partition. The decoration in the revealed chamber is bright and fresh-seeming. The background, like that in the tomb of Thutmose III, represents unrolled papyrus, but it is done here in a golden orange, typical of later burials. Excerpts from the royal *Book of What is in the Dwat*, show (at 2) the king's barque travelling through the underworld with the scarab beetle, Kheper-Re, who presides over the rebirth of the king as he does over the break of day. He is a god of transformations. Below baboons adore the rising sun.

At 3, Hat-hor, wearing her cow horns, offers the *ankh* to the king, who is escorted by the jackal Anubis and Isis, mistress of spells. On the east wall at 4, is the funeral cortège with the sarcophagus being dragged to the tomb by twelve stout bearers.

The north wall shows at 5 the tutor Ay, so schooled in the art of temple politics that he is presented here already as co-regent. On his teenage charge's death, he immediately appointed himself pharaoh. Here Ay touches the king's lips with an adze, opening the mummy's mouth for the breath of life to enter. Nearby, a gangrene-faced Osiris embraces the deceased.

The sarcophagus of pink quartzite is guarded at the corners by Nephthys, with outstretched wings, and Isis. The inner coffin-cases are in Cairo but, exceptionally, the king still lies here in his tomb.

The lid to one side is of granite – a different stone from the sarcophagus – and may have had to serve the turn in the haste of a burial which a conservative reading of the evidence would constrain us to term unexpected. Perhaps even Tut-Ankh-Amun was unaware of what caused the little brown patch on the left side of his skull.

TOMB OF TUTANKHAMUN

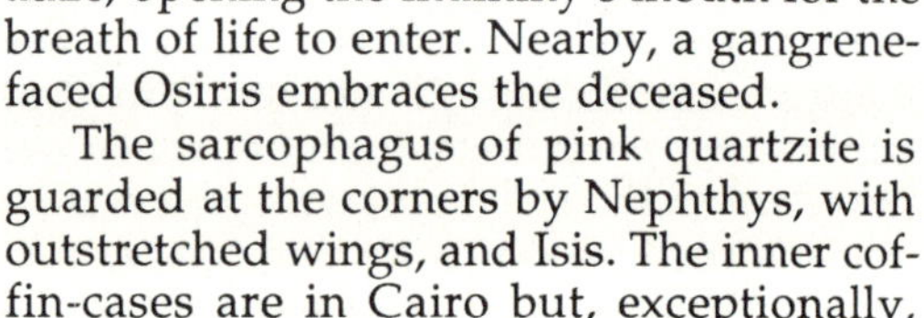

Tomb of Horemheb

(No. 57, 18th/19th dynasties, c.1320BC)

Horemheb was a shrewd and ambitious commoner from the north of Upper Egypt. He became Great Commander of the Army and Vice-regent under Akhenaten. After his patron's death he watched the 18th dynasty tremble and fall and waited to turn its ruin to his own advantage. He waited while the turncoat Ay undermined the political power of the royal family and snatched it for himself with help from the temple. He watched as the priesthood pursued its policy and the state began to fall apart. Little is known of the relationship between the commander and the tutor, except that four years was quite long enough for Horemheb to wait before seizing control. His power base held firm.

He proceeded to restore the temples of Amun and sanctioned the obliteration of all traces of Atenism and its prophet. But at the same time, he made sure to appoint to elevated positions in the hierarchy priests from the army on whose loyalty he could depend.

Although the pharaoh-general rose by the military route to power, Horemheb's twenty-seven year reign was noted more for his piety in restoring temples than for his feats of arms in the imperial cause. Perhaps, after a long career in public service, the commander simply opted for a quiet life.

Horemheb's life after death was ensured by the spells in a formidable tomb which plunges deep into the limestone, to the west of the valley. It is over 300 feet long and rather sparsely decorated. What decoration there is, however, is of excellent workmanship and should be visited by all who are able-bodied.

After two flights of steps, undecorated corridors open into a **Well Room** as in the tomb of Thutmose III.

TOMB OF HOREMHEB

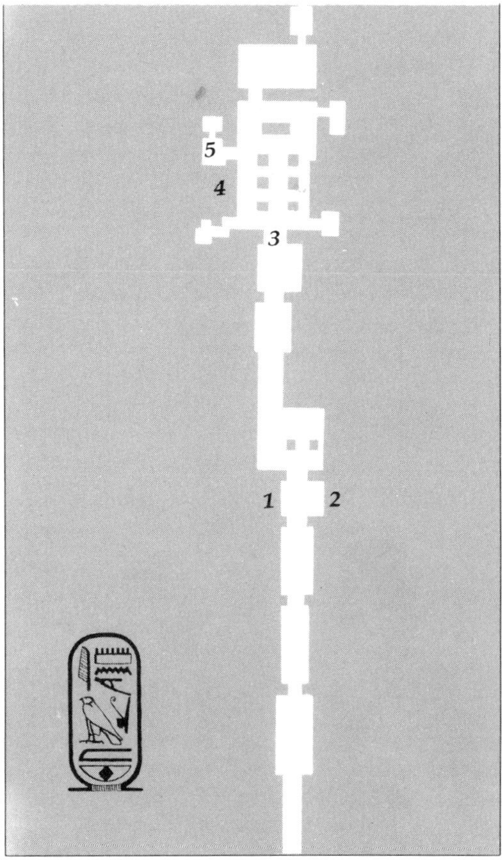

Reliefs show the king being presented to his cousins the gods. On the left wall at *1* are Hat-hor, Osiris with his consort Isis, and Horus. On the right (2) in a similar tableau, Isis is replaced by a rather mean-looking Anubis. From the north-east corner of this, more flights of steps descend, and the corridor opens into a small, undecorated, pillared **Hall**.

The **Antechamber** follows, decorated almost identically to the well room.

The **Burial Chamber** is a six-pillared room with a finely worked red granite sarcophagus at the far end. The decoration was clearly intended to be extensive

Unfinished paintings from the tomb chamber of Horemheb

but bears the marks of work in haste. In some places, the outlines of a figure have not yet been filled in *(see photograph, opposite)*. There are several side chambers. The entrance at **3** is guarded by the goddess of truth, justice and the pure heart, Mât.

The west wall of the burial chamber (**4**) is inscribed with chapters from the *Book of Gates*, and the north shows Osiris in judgement. Here, however, the work is unfinished and the chief artist's corrections are quite obvious.

The tomb painters would work by applying a quarter-inch layer of lime plaster to the smoothed walls. On this they would sometimes impose a standard proportional grid then proceed to sketch in iron oxide, then in lamp-black, the appropriate spells or illustrations.

The borders and upper registers would be executed first. The master craftsman would correct the artisan's work with his red palm-stalk brush and work would start on the infill. The colours remain strong and vivid today because the craftsmen chose mineral-derived pigments which have remained stable.

Red and ochre came from oxide veins in the limestone hills as did white and sometimes black magnesium. Blue and green were manufactured by fusing together sand, salt and copper. Sometimes malachite was ground for green too. A range of intermediate colours was achieved despite technical limitations, through the use of overpainting and washes.

In the upper registers of all four walls, marks indicate the cardinal points of the compass. How this was achieved, so far underground and without the use of magnetic materials, is a subject for speculation.

The little **Side Chamber** at **5** was dedicated to Osiris and shows the god supported by a *djed* pillar – an ancient totem of resurrection and powerful magic for the king's soul *(see photograph, p. 51)*.

Tomb of Ramesses III

(No. 11, 20th dynasty, c. 1165 BC)

Three hundred years and an empire separate the reigns of Thutmose III and Ramesses III. The former brought it into being and the latter was the last to stave off disintegration.

A gulf of style also separates the two periods. We have seen a certain austerity in the earlier tomb; now we are faced with the full-blown baroque of the 20th dynasty.

The tomb is easy to visit. Whereas that of Thutmose was well hidden (before the valley was continually patrolled), that of Ramesses III was marked by four pilasters with bull-headed capitals. It treats the same themes as that of his predecessor but more expansively: the decoration is rich and luxuriant; his tomb seems grandiose to the modern eye.

Excavation was started here for Ramesses' father, Sethnakhte, but work was abandoned when the third corridor broke into an earlier tomb. However, a slight diversion to the right rectified things, and the son's funerary passage was cut a further 200 yards into the rock.

We enter the tomb down a double flight of steps. The slope between was provided for the sliding-in of the sarcophagus. A sun disk containing a scarab

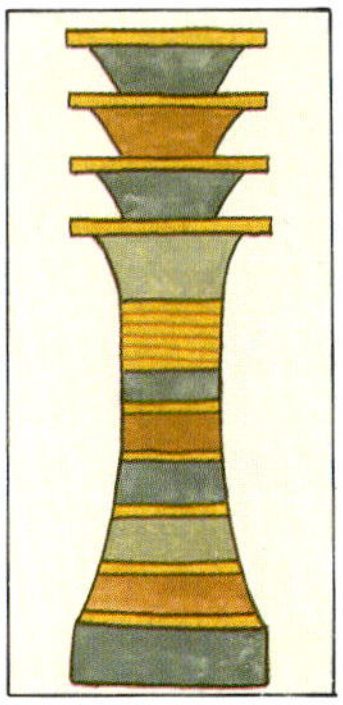

The djed pillar, thought to represent the lopped trunk of a cedar tree, symbolised the possibility of renewed life; it appears typically with Osiris and other funerary deities

and the solar ram appear on the lintel adored by Isis and Nephthys, both protectors of the dead. Beneath the lintel, the various names of Ramesses III are recorded.

Three **corridors** follow. The narrow sections which separate them would have been filled anciently with stout doors.

The walls of the first two corridors are brightly painted with formulae known as the *Litany of Re.* These are the illustrated texts of chants intended to announce to the solar deity that his son has arrived. Although Re was replaced in Thebes as the state god, he retained his power over the dying king. In this matter, above all, we find Egyptians at their most conservative.

Set in the sides of the corridors are **decorated niches**. The chamber to the left in the first corridor shows copious representations of baking and butchery, possibly preparations for a funeral feast. This abundance represents both what the king has achieved and what he expects in the afterlife. The niche to the right shows a riverine funeral courtesy visit to Abydos, a site sacred to Osiris. It is likely that this scene was purely conventional.

Moving to the second corridor, the chambers on the left contain, first, at **1**, Hapi, the hermaphrodite Nile god (note the incongruous dug and beard), who offers his abundance to seven demiurges wearing ears of corn and representing the harvest. At **2**, the chamber is filled with protective spirits making offerings for the king. At **3**, Ramesses III appears as a bull with seven cows: at **4**, on the entrance to the chamber, are two representations of aspects of the pharaoh's soul standing guard; they bear wands topped with the heads of the king's ancestors. The fourth niche shows harpists with the words they sing to announce the arrival of the king to the gods.

The four niches on the right of the second corridor make provision for the future.

Ramesses III wearing the Atef crown of Osiris

At **5**, the might of the pharaoh is symbolised by his quivers, bows and arrows, and his standards. The act of shooting (as may be seen on the walls at Medinet Habu and the Ramesseum) was a magical act, demonstrating the king's virility and his protection of the gods and the state. At **6**, pictures of luxurious furniture and ornaments demonstrate the state to which the pharaoh aspires. It was thought that, should the grave be robbed, representations such as these would ensure enough material ease when the king reached the other side. The third chamber on the right of this corridor shows the king sailing placidly through the New Kingdom paradise – the Fields of Reeds (*Yaru* in ancient Egyptian). Idealised agricultural scenes signify regularity and plenty. In the last niche (**7**) Osiris, prince of paradise, appears in twelve shapes.

The corridor debouches into a small anteroom. Here the walls are illustrated

TOMB OF RAMESSES III

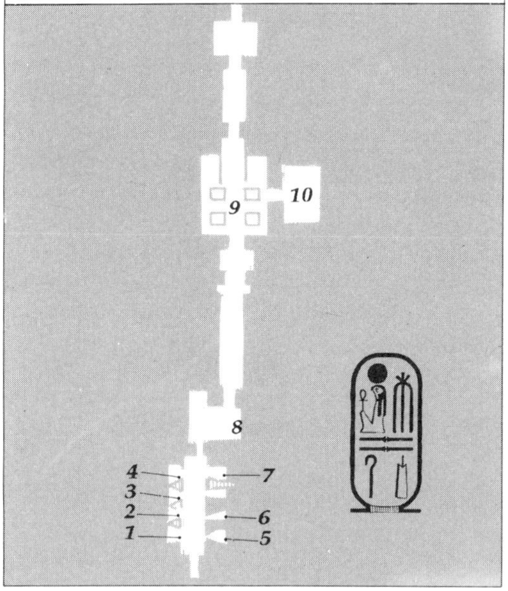

with pictures of the pharaoh offering to several guardian deities of the underworld, including Anubis and Osiris at *8*. Notice that Osiris is, as nearly always, in the form of a mummy, but bearing the flail and crook of royal authority. His face is greenish-black, indicating both that he is dead and promises new life. It was here that the diversion of the tomb plan was found to be necessary, so we turn right and left to continue into the tomb.

The third corridor, decorated with part of the *Litany of Re,* shows the sun god progressing through the netherworld.

A small square **Well Room** with Hathor at the entrance, is painted on the left with pictures of Horus the Younger (son of Osiris) and his descendants (the early mythical kings of Egypt). The well has been bridged for your convenience.

On the right wall, Osiris again appears, with his royal regalia. Taken together, these scenes indicate the intimate, family relationship between the rulers of heaven, earth and the underworld.

There follows a hall with four pillars (*9*) which are decorated with offering scenes to Re-Harakhte (falcon-headed sun god), Kheper-Re (with a scarab on his shoulders, here representing solar renewal or rebirth), and Atum, an early creation god in human form, holding an *ankh*.

The walls are inscribed with part of the *Book of Gates,* which describes stages of the journey of the sun – and, by implication, the king – through the hours of the night. The gate of each hour is guarded with fierce snakes, and black demons threaten to turn his breath to fire or hang him upside down and make him eat excrement. But the king, fortified by his elaborate preparations, sails through on his barque undisturbed by the sirens of chaos.

The gallery-room to the right at *10*, continues the journey, and concludes with the king before Osiris the judge. Ramesses presents a feather, here a symbol of a pure heart, to Osiris. In the pharaoh's case, however, the judgement is something of a formality. He is, after all, himself a god.

From the pillared hall, steps descend steeply to the damaged burial chamber (currently out of bounds during restoration). It is empty, since the sarcophagus has been removed to Paris. The sarcophagus, too, is empty: its former contents now lie in the Egyptian Museum.

Several other tombs in the valley are usually open to visitors. If the prospect of the climb to Thutmose III's eyrie seems daunting, the burial of **Amenhotep II** (Amenophis II) *Number 35* – is decorated with similar restraint. The tombs of **Ramesses VI** – *Number 9* – and **Ramesses IX** – *Number 6* – show off the florid style of the later Ramessides to advantage.

A late afternoon visit is recommended, otherwise the continual filing in and out of marshalled groups proves a tourist distraction.

The Valley of the Queens at the southern end of the Theban range

Valley of the Queens

Branching southwest from the Antiquities Department's office, a tarmac road winds steeply into the heart of the Theban hills.

Here is the Valley of the Queens – a neatly complementary title, but something of a misnomer. Many burials here are of princes or minor royalty of both sexes.

Simple shaft burials of ladies of royal lineage were carried out here in the 18th dynasty but it was only in the time of Seti I *(1309-1291 BC)* and later that more extensive use was made of the area. The first queen of major rank to be buried here was Nefertari, wife of Ramesses II *(1290-1224 BC)*. In the 20th dynasty, queens and princesses of every degree were regularly interred in this valley, and Ramesses III had quite elaborate tombs built for his sons Khaemweset and Amun–Hir–Khopshef.

Many of the score of tombs dotted about this barren hillside are simple caves, carved crudely from the rock and plainly decorated, if at all. Others display interesting wall paintings, but these are often in poor condition.

Of those which are graced with paint, some have been closed by the Antiquities Department: the mass perspiration and promiscuous fingers of some eighty million trippers have caused whole sections to peel away from the wall.

Archaeologists have begun painstaking and difficult restoration work to stick some of the tiny flakes of paint back on the rock walls. But there is no guarantee of success. Pigments that remained bright for millennia have faded before a generation of mass tourism.

Tomb of Tyti *(No. 52)*

This tomb is simple in design but extensively decorated. Tyti was the wife of a latterday Ramesses who reigned towards the end of the twelfth century BC. At this time, the dynasty of the Ramessides was fast losing its grip on the Egyptian body politic. At the same time, provision for the afterlife grew more luxuriant and baroque.

That the Tomb of Queen Tyti is a royal burial is clear from its scale and the luxury of its adornment. It is also typical of its period in that its corridors have no niches and there is a shrine with three side chapels, so the plan resembles a celtic cross.

At the entrance, on the door-jambs, the remains of the titles of the Queen may be found. On either side of the walls of the first corridor the goddess Mât is shown with wings, kneeling and attesting to the purity of the queen's soul.

At *1*, the dead queen adores the bald Ptah in his shrine and Re-Harakhte, the royal sun-god. Opposite, at *2*, Tyti adores Thoth, Atum (as creator) and lesser deities who will act as her guides through the *Dwat*.

Inside the shrine, a motley crew of demi-gods guards the doorways of the underworld. A jackal and a lion menace the intruder at *3* while baboons and a monkey drawing a bow posture at *4*. The function of the squatting boy is unclear, although he may represent a fresh start. At any rate, the texts in this chamber reassure the lady that her clean heart will see her through the dark night of the soul.

The barque of her *ba* is shown on each side of the entrance to the rear chamber at *5*. Remnants of a scene with the deceased before Osiris are just visible at *6*. Queen Tyti appears in an unusually landscaped picture at *7*, adoring the horned Hat-hor in the mountains of the west and drinking reviving water offered by a tree-spirit.

The chamber on the left contained the queen's sarcophagus.

If there is time, a brief visit to the nearby tombs of two sons of Ramesses III is worthwhile. They are the tombs of princes **Khaemweset** *(No. 44)* and **Amun-Hir-Khopshef** *(No. 55)*. In both, the king leads his boys to the underworld, interceding on their behalf. In the latter a pickled foetus of unknown origin has given rise to much macabre speculation.

Hat-hor emerges from the western hills to welcome the queen to the Dwat

TOMB OF TYTI

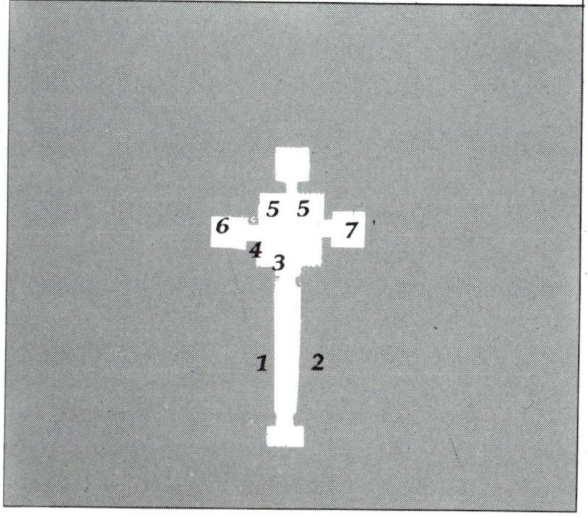

The Book of the Dead and the Life to Come

The *Book of the Dead* is not so much a book as a series of spells or incantations, designed to assist the deceased in his passage through the Dwat or underworld and to help him arrive safely in the Fields of Reeds. The Book underlines the importance of the written word to the Egyptians in this most vital of undertakings.

Different copies of the Book comprise a varying number of chapters, some of them elaborations on well-treated themes, some very arcane, but all aimed at preserving and promoting elements of the immortal soul.

Diligent scholars have discovered inconsistencies and contradictions in the *Book of the Dead* as scholars do with religious documents. The spells envisage at least four types of afterlife. In one, that part of the soul called the *akh* would become a star. This belief, shared by the Greeks and Romans, is very ancient indeed, dating back well before historical times.

A second scenario for the departed is that his *ba* – another aspect of his soul – would spend eternity circling the globe in the solar boat of Re. This idea was most fully developed in the age of the pyramids, when king worship was promoted in connection with an uncluttered cult of the sun.

Elsewhere we learn that the successful *ba* will be living contentedly in the Fields of Reeds, doing a little placid agricultural work to sustain him over the aeons. The *ba* was also able to return like a ghost to haunt the people and places he had become attached to in his mortal lifetime.

A less attractive eternity awaited the *ka*, which was destined to abide forever with the earthly remains of the deceased or his statue. It was for the *ka* that relatives of the dead, or their appointed priests, brought funerary food offerings: it was thought these would fortify him in his endless vigil.

The Book is copiously illustrated with scenes of the trials and perils to be encountered on the way to paradise or extinction.

Judgement scene from the Book of the Dead (Papyrus of Hunefer)

courtesy of the British Museum

Our first evidence of the Book is from magical texts carved on the inside of the early pyramids at Saqqara. It developed a solar aspect during the Old Kingdom and, by the late Middle Kingdom a quite elaborate myth of Osiris had become established.

A favourite scene from the *Book of the Dead* shows the deceased led before Osiris by supporting deities. His heart is then weighed in the balance against the feather of truth. If the life is found wanting, quick extinction awaits in the form of a frightful chimera with lion's jaws. Osiris is president of this tribunal, but the decision is ratified by forty-two judges – one for each aspect of the deceased's former character.

Throughout the early dynasties, most Egyptians had nothing to look forward to after death. The spirit world was a club with restricted membership. At first, only the king would cross that ultimate threshhold. But cosmologies have the convenient habit of changing according to social circumstances in the world of men. As the power of the early dynastic kings became more dependent on their political supporters, the viziers and nomarchs demanded and achieved a place in the sun. By the time of the Middle Kingdom, the nobility were regularly interred in great splendour, near the tombs of the pharaoh.

A gradual democratization of religious experience took place. During the Old Kingdom, texts from the Book were reserved for royal burials, but by the Ramesside period, they found their way onto the chapel walls of commoners (the tomb of Sennujem displays many texts and scenes of this type).

By the late New Kingdom, the burials of even humble folk demonstrate that they too looked forward to a life of bliss in the Fields of Reeds. Those who had any means at all would have at least a papyrus roll with passages from the Book placed in their coffin. These were mass-produced and had blanks, like a standard contract, where the deceased's relatives might reverently fill in the name.

Anubis embalms Sennujem in a scene from the Book of the Dead

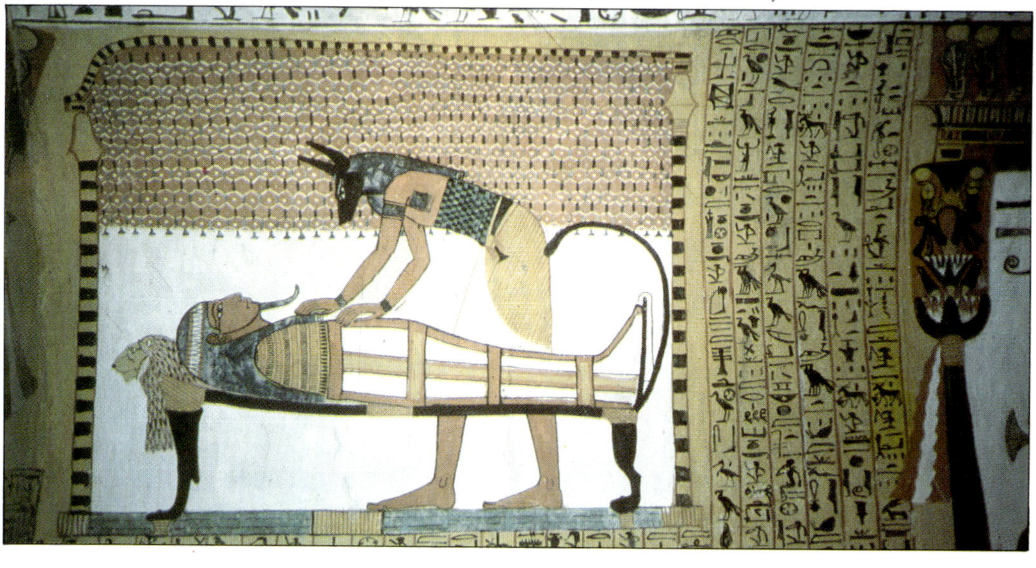

Tombs of the Nobles

The village of Gurna is scattered over the foothills of the Theban hills. Tombs of the nobles riddle the limestone beneath. The two share many secrets. Although over four hundred burials have been discovered to date, a *Gurnawy* in his cups will hint at hidden places known only to the few. Most tombs were plundered in antiquity, but some believe there is still scope for the modern grave-robber.

The Nobles' tombs are simple affairs; most of them were excavated roughly in the shape of an *ankh*, symbolising eternal life. There is usually a dedicatory chapel followed by a short corridor and a shrine with a statue of the deceased. The burial would be at the bottom of a long shaft.

The tombs of the kings served a vital purpose of state; the themes on the walls were treated conservatively. So the king appears somewhat remote and abstract in his divinity. But the passing of a nobleman or woman would make no difference to the harvest or the fate of Egypt, so we find more style in the decoration of these lesser burials; less slavish copying-out of formulae. The viziers and scribes are shown in the diversity of their mortal activity and are for that more recognisably human.

These tombs are less daunting (and, to be frank, less spooky) than the royal burials. Here we find a family scene, there the gathering-in of a harvest. From the perspective of a television culture the representations seem almost realistic.

But we should guard against reading too much into these decorations merely because we relate more readily to the freer style. The drawings were for magical and religious purposes and not done as an exercise in self-expression. However, these tomb walls remain an encyclopaedia of historical information, unrivalled in the ancient world, which archaeologists are still striving to understand.

TOMB-CHAPEL OF NAKHT

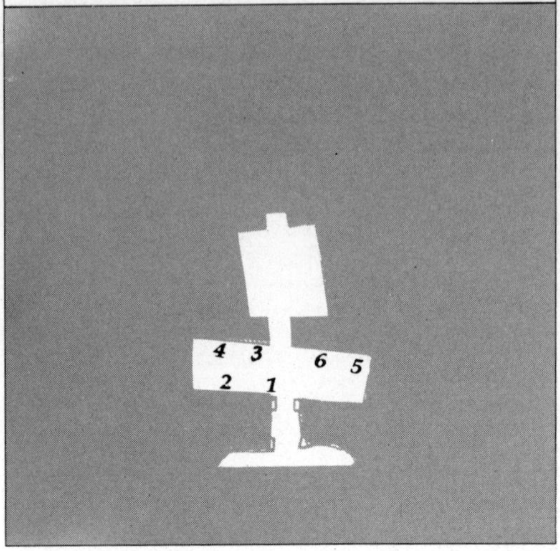

Tomb-Chapel of Nakht

(No. 52)

The nobleman to whom this tomb belongs was a high official serving Thutmose IV. He held several offices, notably Keeper of the King's Granaries, Master of the Vineyards and Astronomer Royal.

The visitor is welcomed to the first room, the chapel, by an offering: Nakht and his wife, a Chantress of Amun, stand before a table at *1*, piled high with perfectly-formed food-items. The baskets of grapes, however, have been left in outline. The food is an offering to Amun, no doubt in anticipation of eternal favours in return.

Most of the decoration in the chapel is lively and delights the eye. There is a harvest scene, a banquet and a hunting scene, all quite jolly and unfunereal. But the scenes are in fact highly conventional, and our fascination with the incidental detail should not obscure the special purpose which they serve.

While it is true that Nakht was Keeper of the Granaries, the toy-town scene at 2 in which flax and wheat are harvested, is

A bouquet for a nobleman from his son

Pressing the vintage to supply Nakht in the afterlife

not so much a record of the official's life, rather an invocation of the Fields of Reeds which are his eternal hope. Naturally, having led a life of some luxury on earth, Nakht would expect a little help in the afterworld. Thus, he is shown doing a minimum of physical activity – he plucks an ear of corn here, supervises the ploughing with a word there, while all around him scurry fellaheen doing the dirty work.

His view of the ideal reveals a structured, orderly society with the perfect corn springing for ever and ever and plenty of willing labour to reap and measure, winnow and pack the grain. But the artists have provided for the labourers too: note in the lower register how a hand tipples from a water-skin cooling in a tree.

The luxurious banquet at **3**, with singing and dancing, seems impossibly out of place for a funeral wake; even more so when we note the deceased is enjoying it too. This was clearly an imagined scene. The representation is invocatory, conjuring up good times for the astronomer in his life among the stars – or wherever he might find himself.

At **4**, Nakht's son brings him flowers symbolising the awakening of the spirit. Attractive naked girls tootle on pipes and another plucks at a curious lute-harp, swaying in time to the music. Here, the divine harmony required by convention has the distinctly sensual overtones of a fleshly paradise. More underdressed maidservants offer perfume to their overdressed mistresses (as ever, clothing was a sign of rank). The chattering women at the banquet wear cakes of perfumed grease in their coif-fures. These would melt during the evening and dribble aromatically down their necks.

At **5** , we see more of the good things of life that Nakht wants for himself and his family. Here is a vineyard, with men gathering the grapes. Their hair resembles the fruit they pluck. In the wine

A magical net ensures dominion for the nobleman beyond the grave

press, men are merrily trampling the vintage. The wine-jars wait above. This picture also works on a symbolic level. The change of consciousness brought about by intoxication seems to have represented the release of the mind in the world beyond the west.

Below, more of nature's abundance is brought into the service of Nakht. Ducks are caught in a net-trap, plucked and eviscerated then hung up to dry. Possibly this scene also signifies the triumph of Nakht over chaos and his enemies *(photograph, above).*

At 6 Nakht goes a-hunting. In the marshes, the official takes time off from the office for more primitive and manly pursuits. He hunts fowl and small animals with a throwing stick. Along for the trip are his son and his wife who clings submissively to her man's leg.

Some researchers say this kind of expedition rarely took place in the 18th dynasty. The tableau, again conventional, has much more to do with vitality and potency in the afterlife than blood-lust in this. The chantress is wearing a particularly elaborate wig which, in Egyptian iconography, suggests a different sport entirely.

However, a spoil-sport intruder, probably with a grudge against Nakht, has scratched out his eyes and broken his boomerang. Even in their pettinesses, the Egyptians demonstrated an unshakeable conviction in the material reality beyond the grave.

The shrine, its sides undecorated, has a niche at the far end which once contained a statue of the dead man.

The *ka* of Nakht, if it still inhabits this statue, now faces a somewhat gloomier eternity than that anticipated on the chapel walls. It was torpedoed by the Imperial German Navy in 1917 while being shipped to a wealthy American collector and lies at the bottom of the Atlantic Ocean.

Tomb-Chapel of Ramose

(No. 55)

This tomb-chapel was conceived on a grander scale than that of Nakht. Ramose was grander, too, holding two of the state's most estimable offices: Governor of Thebes and Vizier of Egypt. The thirty-two papyrus bud pillars of the chapel offer something of the cool elegance of the colonnade at Luxor Temple and remind us of the dignity of its owner.

Ramose was from Memphis. His brother, Amenhotep, was Commissioner for Public Works of that city. The painstaking raised relief of this tomb has a delicacy of style which may derive from a Memphite school.

Whatever their ancestry, reliefs on the wall near the entrance are masterpieces of the limestone medium. Sparely highlighted with a little touch of kohl around the eyes, the representations of Ramose and his wife at *1* rival those in the tomb of Tî at Saqqara in detail and finesse *(photograph opposite).*

To the right of the entrance, Ramose is shown paying his respects to Amenhotep IV. This was the original throne name of the pharaoh who became Akhenaten. Both the monarch and his vizier are shown in a traditional way. The orderly proportion betrays nothing of the political imbroglio that was going on above ground.

But on the opposite wall at 2 an aesthetic thunderbolt has struck. An unfinished wall-painting shows the same king, but a little older and much odder.

Some people have seen in this pot-bellied, spindly-limbed gawk a 'naturalistic' portrayal of the great monotheist. If he really were that unusual in physical appearance, what extraordinary will-power the man must have possessed. The pharaoh should be perfect; in earlier times the ill-favoured king would have been put to death.

It is more likely that the 'Amarna' style represented an attempt to avoid the conventions which the priests had hallowed, rather than a conscious attempt at naturalism. The vizier (whom the king showers with gold in the manner of an Arabian oil potentate), is also depicted in similar eccentric brush-strokes, although much smaller; the convention that shows rank by size remains curiously unchallenged. At 3, the *Aten* – the sun disk – extends rays with little hands that support the pharaoh and offer blessings to the king and Queen Nefertiti.

On the side wall at **4** we return to a more recognisable style, although the treatment is also a little wild. The funeral procession of Ramose is shown, with hired mourners bursting tears in all directions, swooning with emotion and heaping dirt on their heads. A group of men carry food-offerings covered with leaves to keep them cool for the *ka* of Ramose.

The inner chamber, with eight unfinished columns, is undecorated although Ramose is shown adoring the *Aten* at the entrance. Burial shafts here and in the shrine at the far end lead to tombs which were discovered empty.

If you have time, you might care to visit the adjacent tombs of **Userhet** *(No. 56)*, a Royal Scribe under Amenhotep II and that of **Khaemhet** *(No. 57)*, Master of the Granaries under Amenhotep III.

TOMB-CHAPEL OF RAMOSE

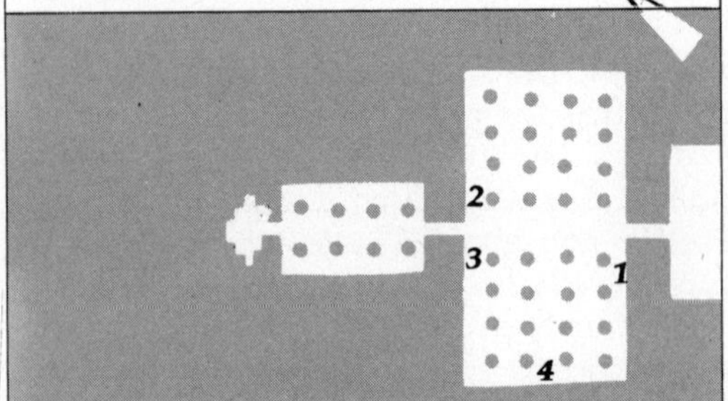

Finely-carved portraits of Ramose and his wife from the chapel of Ramose

Tomb of Sennujem

(No. 1)

The tomb of Sennujem is to be found on the slopes of the *Gurn*, just above the ruined village at Deir El Medina *(see map page 10)*. This village was home to some eighty families of necropolitan builders and decorators for much of the New Kingdom.

Gangs of scribes, painters, porters, cooks, potters and labourers would work ten-day shifts in the tombs, with a day off between shifts. Accommodation was simple, but adequate, and payment was in kind. These workers were not slaves, but neither had they much choice in the matter of a career.

The craftsmen of the village were known as *Servants in the Place of Truth* – the Necropolis. Their status was relatively low in the ancient Egyptian scheme of things; they were thought of as craftsmen rather than artists. But the standard of their work speaks for itself.

The village was closed and guarded to make sure no news of the whereabouts of rich burials should leak out. This policy was almost entirely unsuccessful as any resident of nearby Gurna could testify.

Sennujem was of some consequence among the Servants in the Place of Truth, and his burial bears all the hallmarks of this advantage. In particular, no-one robbed his tomb. Assuming that intelligence regarding the whereabouts of fresh mummies came from this village, it seems a burial in the family was protected from indignities suffered by the corpses of the great and the good. Sennujem's basic tomb furniture may be seen in the Egyptian Museum.

Simple in arrangement, the tomb is far from plain. Expert artists have obviously lent a hand here. A steep, straight flight of steps next curves to the left and ends in a simple rectangular chamber with a vaulted roof.

The roof displays favourite scenes from the *Book of the Dead*, showing the *ba* of Sennujem travelling in a boat piloted by Thoth, and the Gates of the West being opened. These scenes of beyond the grave are typical of the burials of the later Ramesside period.

At **1**, Sennujem's mummy is shown in place, guarded by Isis and Nephthys transformed into birds. Under the *ished* tree at **2**, a cat wrestles a snake to death, symbolising the vanquishing of evil forces. More demons may be seen at **3**.

At **4**, Anubis is shown embalming the corpse *(photograph, page 67)* then leading him to Osiris. The King of the Dead himself, in his usual mummy manifestation, stands by a table flanked by two eyes of Horus which signify the best of all offerings. At **5**, Sennujem and his wife make a handsome couple.

The bucolic tableau at **6** is set in the now familiar Fields of Reeds *(photograph opposite)*. Unlike the magnificent Nakht, Sennujem is not averse to a doing a spot of

TOMB OF SENNUJEM

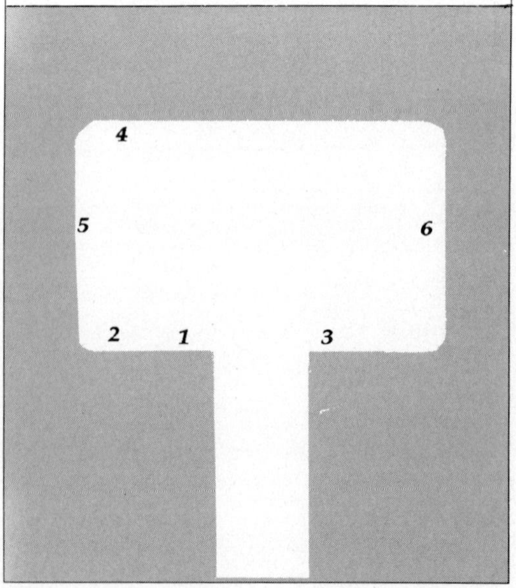

Sennujem and his wife reap the rewards of a lifetime of public service : an eternity of bucolic bliss in the Fields of Reeds – the Egyptian Elysium.

ploughing himself, while his wife follows, scattering the seed. Even so, they hardly seemed dressed for the occasion.

This rendition of paradise offers us interesting information about earthly agriculture in the 19th dynasty: barley is being harvested in the upper register (the ancient Egyptians cut off the heads) and, below that, flax (which was pulled up by the roots).

A papyrus marsh is also shown underneath. The plant was made into the familiar woven paper, a basic medium for communication and an important Egyptian monopoly for much of antiquity.

Papyrus was also made into ropes, mats, sandals and even boats, adequate for everyday use on the Nile.

The outdoor scene is a lively affair, but does little to relieve the claustrophobic effect of this tomb. The vaulted roof gives the whole chamber the atmosphere of a coffin.

Nearby, capped by elongated pyramids, are other tombs of Servants in the Place of Truth which are worth a visit if you have the time.

Also recommended to the less hurried visitor is the small Ptolemaic temple at **Deir El Medina**, a short walk west of the village ruins. It stands almost complete and rivals that of Queen Hatshepsut in its setting.

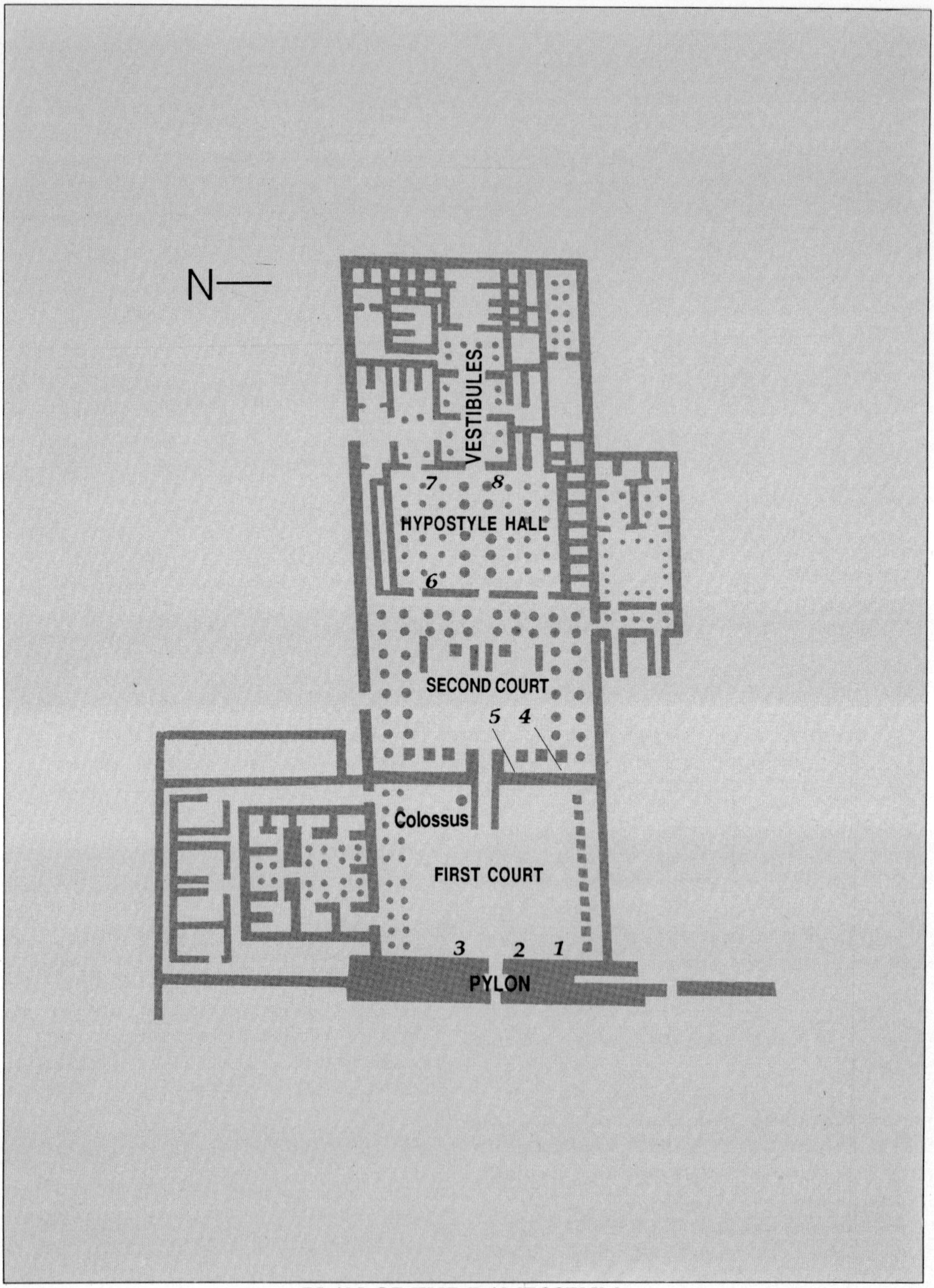

PLAN OF THE RAMESSEUM

The Ramesseum

This temple takes its name from King Ramesses II, commonly styled 'the Great'. He was a pharaoh in the grand manner, his splendour rivalling that of the pyramid builders of the Old Kingdom. His monuments were many, and prodigious was the industry of his scribes in glorifying the few military engagements which this long-lived monarch actually undertook.

Enter the Ramesseum from the north. The original approach, through the great pylon, was from the east but the way is now blocked with fallen masonry.

This temple suffered, like that of Amenhotep III, from lack of foresight. It was built on ground too often flooded by the Nile to fulfil the promise of its official title: *The Palace of Millions of Years of King Ramesses II.*

In principle, temples were designed to last for ever. Built of stone (the hardest material available), they were thus distinguished from the mud brick dwellings of antiquity, of which there is now no trace beneath the fields.

The mighty, fallen shoulders of Ramesses II

Beyond the temple walls, throughout the fertile flood-plain, the untiring seasons ran in their perpetual cycles of growth and decay. Only the gods remained unchanged.

All that lived and moved was ordered by the gods, who were worshipped as various aspects of the one life force. On them depended the sprouting of seed, the harvest's abundance and the welfare of the land. A temple was designed to protect and propitiate the gods, who were vital to the maintenance of life and order among men.

The theoretical basis of the structure was sound enough, but in this case its physical foundations were quite undermined. The mortuary temple of Ramesses the Great is now in a sorry state: broken columns litter the ground, its pylons have crumbled, the statues of the pharaoh fallen.

In particular, enormous fragments of a colossus lie smashed into the second court *(photograph, this page).*

On seeing a fanciful engraving of this statue, the English poet, Percy Shelley, was inspired to write these lines:

I met a traveller from an antique land,
Who said: Two vast and trunkless legs of stone
Stand in the desert... Near them , on the sand,
Half sunk, a shattered visage lies, whose frown,
And wrinkled lip, and sneer of cold command,
Tell that the sculptor well those passions read
Which yet survive, stamped on these lifeless things,
The hand that mocked them and the heart that fed.
And on the pedestal these words appear:
'My name is Ozymandias, king of kings:
Look on my works, ye Mighty, and despair!'
Nothing beside remains. Round the remains
of that colossal wreck, boundless and bare,
The lone and level sands stretch far away.

The Osiride colonnade in the second court of the Ramesseum

Even less remained in 1816 after the circus strongman-cum-archaeological entrepreneur, Giovanni Belzoni, connived with the British Consul, a Mr. Henry Salt, to haul a second statue back to England, where it now weighs heavily on the foundations of the British Museum. The colossus now *in situ* was about sixty feet high; seated in its barge on its way from Aswan, it would have displaced nearly one thousand tons. Destroyed as it is, the granite sculpture still displays a flawless finish that leaves the modern artisan in awe. So much time and effort went into its quarrying, cutting, polishing and transport: this colossus represents absolute power in a way no monument of our own age can approach.

But power has a tendency to ride rough-shod over facts, and Ramesses II galloped over a good deal of them in his time. For example, on the inside of the first pylon *(best viewed around noon)* reliefs offer a blazing account of a battle with a 'vile Asiatic foe'.

First Pylon: The Battle of Kadesh

This pylon gives a partial account of Ramesses II's most notable victory (notable chiefly as a propaganda coup because it was not a victory at all). The objective was the city of Kadesh in the eastern Levant, where the Beka'a valley debouches onto the Syrian plain. When Ramesses II assumed office, the Levantine hinterland was dominated by Hittites. These warlike Caucasians had established a mountain stronghold in Anatolia, where they grew ever bolder in their ambition. Their armies swarmed into the fertile crescent, lay waste the cities of Mitanni and razed the towers of Babylon.

They disputed the northern Levant with Egypt. The battle for Kadesh was to be the occasion for Ramesses to 'rage like a panther', as the formula put it, and humble their o'erweening empire. It took place in the fourth year of his reign c.1285 BC.

On the left tower of the pylon, at *1* the army strikes camp. Ramesses confers with his princes and the horses are fed. At *2 (lower register)*, captured Syrians are being tortured for their news. And the news they give out is what the king expected. The craven enemy have fled; a little mopping up is all that is required and victory will be his.

But treachery was afoot. Rashly believing the tale of the Syrian agents, his majesty pressed on with his bodyguard towards the river valley. Hardly had the company set up the king's pavilion than a host of Hittites, armed to the teeth, charged from behind a hill where they had been hiding. Ramesses was trapped. The division of Ptah was half a day's march away, and the Hittites were on familiar ground.

On the southern tower at *3*, however, Ramesses II, inflated by artistic convention to gigantic proportions, draws his mighty bow (with one sure finger) and strikes terror into the hearts of the enemy whom his lusty stallions trample on the ground. Ramesses appears twice, but no Egyptian apart from the god-king is shown in combat. One servile account relates that Ramesses charged alone five times into the thick of battle and set a hundred thousand warriors to flight.

THE EASTERN MEDITERRANEAN *c 1250 BC*

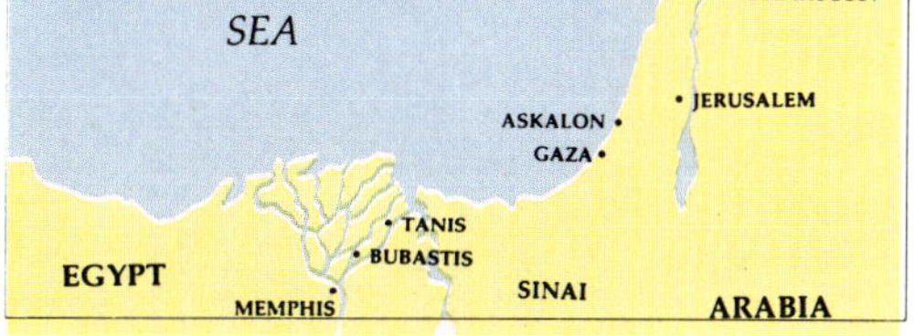

Second Court

More in this vein is shown on the inside of the remaining wall of the second court. Behind the battered Osiride colonnade at **4** the pharaoh spreads panic among the enemy troops. A lion, evoking the monarch's wrath, lopes at his side. (It is carved between the king's quiver and the wheel-axle of his chariot.) Again Ramesses is shown with his bow drawn, frozen in the moment of maximum force. In his mortuary temple he has become the principle of kingly power, his dominion is maintained forever.

This invasion of the sacred, inner parts of the temple with war reliefs represents a departure from tradition. It was the legitimate function of the pylon to keep out impudent foreigners, it offered a graphic warning to any who thought of attacking Egypt and her shrines. Equally, the pharaoh's role was champion of the resident deities and defender of the faith. With Ramesses II's monuments, however, that role seems to have degenerated into an orgy of public self-glorification that knew no decent bounds. The dead weight of political power disturbed the spirit and balance of the creator gods.

However, as a record of style and attitude, this relief has much to offer *(illustration below).* The Asians rush pell mell for the safety of their fortress at **5**. Horses, chariots and men flounder helplessly in the River Orontes. A regiment is drawn up in ranks on the far bank. They seem incapable of defending themselves, although some are helping their wounded comrades climb from the water. The Hittites wear rounded helmets that cover the ears, and are armed with staves; their leaders are dressed in long, rather narrow striped robes, which must have restricted their mobility in combat.

This somewhat boschian turmoil involves a radical departure from the artistic conventions of the New Kingdom. Although the king's horses are done traditionally, the legs fanning out in confident symmetery, the proportions of the enemy are all over the place, their ground is unsure and they lack the dignity of civilised portrayal. It is certain that all this was approved by the king. This is how he showed himself and his enemy to Egypt and the gods.

The Battle of Kadesh, according to Ramesses II

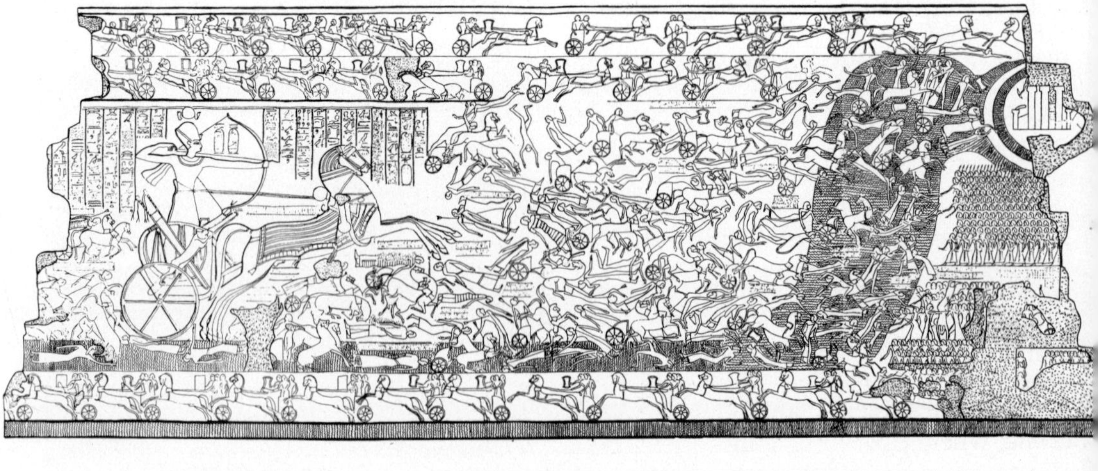

But it was a lie. Accounts of the same battle discovered in Anatolia tell a very different story: Kadesh stood firm against pharaoh and remained in the hands of Metwallis, the Hittite king. Ramesses was forced to withdraw to Aba (near modern Damascus), and, flushed out from there by Metwallis, ran in panic for the Nile.

On the other hand, the Hittite god-kings were themselves no strangers to the art of boasting. On the whole, scholarly opinion inclines to the view that the Asians won on points.

In the event, after fifteen years of threats and posturing, prudence prevailed, and Ramesses signed a treaty with the Hittites (a copy of which, in cuneiform, was discovered on clay tablets at Boghazköy in Turkey in 1907). Metwallis' successor, Khatusilis, cemented the union by sending a daughter to be married to his brother in war. Many versions of the treaty exist, one *(see page 36)* at Karnak, another at Abu Simbel .

The second court is also in ruin, apart from the five statues of the king as Osiris. Held across his mummiform breast are the crook and flail of royal authority. Ramesses is shown as Osiris because it was though his spirit would partake of the nature of Osiris (by tradition the first lord of Egypt) when it entered the underworld. The individual monarch becomes one with the principle of kingship. In a mortuary temple, the pharaoh has joined his fellow gods, and is worshipped along with them.

Hypostyle Hall

Moving westwards, and upwards, we come into the columned hall. There are 48 sandstone pillars in six rows. This marks the beginning of the less public part of the temple. Alas, even here (at *6*) the shouts of war disturb the palace of eternity. Again the scene is Asia, this time in Palestine, where the king and his sons storm

Morning in the Hypostyle Hall at the Ramesseum

the fortress of Dhapur. Notice the effective use of shields and siege-huts.

At *7*, Amun bestows royalty on the king. Below in a row are some of Ramesses' sons (there were over 100 of them). Behind the god stands his consort, Mut. The whole panel *(photograph below)* may be taken as a hieroglyph of the king's legitimacy.

Vestibules

Two small halls with columns follow. These would have served as vestibules for the gathering of offerings to Amun.

The first (sometimes called the **Astronomical Room**) has a ceiling showing the divisions of the day and the night, together with the guardians of the hours travelling in their barques. Ancient Egyptians divided both night and day into twelve equal segments throughout the year, so the hour was a flexible unit.

At *8* the numbers of years of the king's reign are being written on the leaves of the *ished* tree by Thoth and Atum – an ancient creator and solar deity. Sheshet, the goddess of measure, lends a hand. On the east wall, there are processional scenes with boats. As is usual in Egyptian temples, the ceiling still bears a little of its original colour.

These rooms used to lead to the **sanctuary**, but this is now completely destroyed.

Around the remains of this temple, crumbled structures of mud brick mark the site of store-rooms and quarters for priests and servants of the god's household. A mortuary temple had to be well provided for if the pharaoh's cult was to continue for ever, as it was required to do. Vast resources were allotted by the treasury in perpetuity for the maintenance of worship.

Alas, even so great a king as Ramesses II could not provide for the straitened circumstances that overtook the Ramesside dynasty, nor could he unleash his arrows against the ultimate indifference of time.

Amun bestows royalty on Ramesses II

The second court

Medinet Habu from the fields to the south

Mortuary Temple of Ramesses III at Medinet Habu

Of all the ancient buildings in Luxor and on the west bank, the mortuary temple of Ramesses III is the best preserved and best illustrates the basic ideas that underlie the design of these vast religious foundations.

Its form is more integrated than the temple of Luxor and less cluttered than those of Karnak. It is the classic Egyptian temple and, unlike its overrun cousins on the east bank, grows quiet towards sunset when one may fancy it still radiates some of the religious conviction which invested its construction. For this was a profoundly sacred place – at once an offering by the living king to his deified counterpart in the afterlife and a magical representation of the universe of man, wherein ritual and sacrifice would ensure the continued order of existence.

The temple grounds are encircled by a vast perimeter wall, built of sun-dried mud brick; the main buildings are completely guarded from the profane world by massive stone walls. Formerly approached by its own canal, which ended near the great eastern gate, the edifice must have overawed approaching pilgrims, framed as it is by the vast natural pyramid of the Gurn mountain to the north-west.

The Eastern Gate

Today, the visitor enters through the only feature of the whole complex which is not met with elsewhere in Egypt: the daunting, crenellated eastern gate, which looks more like a crusader castle than the doorway to a temple. It is possible that Ramesses III, or his architects, copied this design from fortresses encountered during

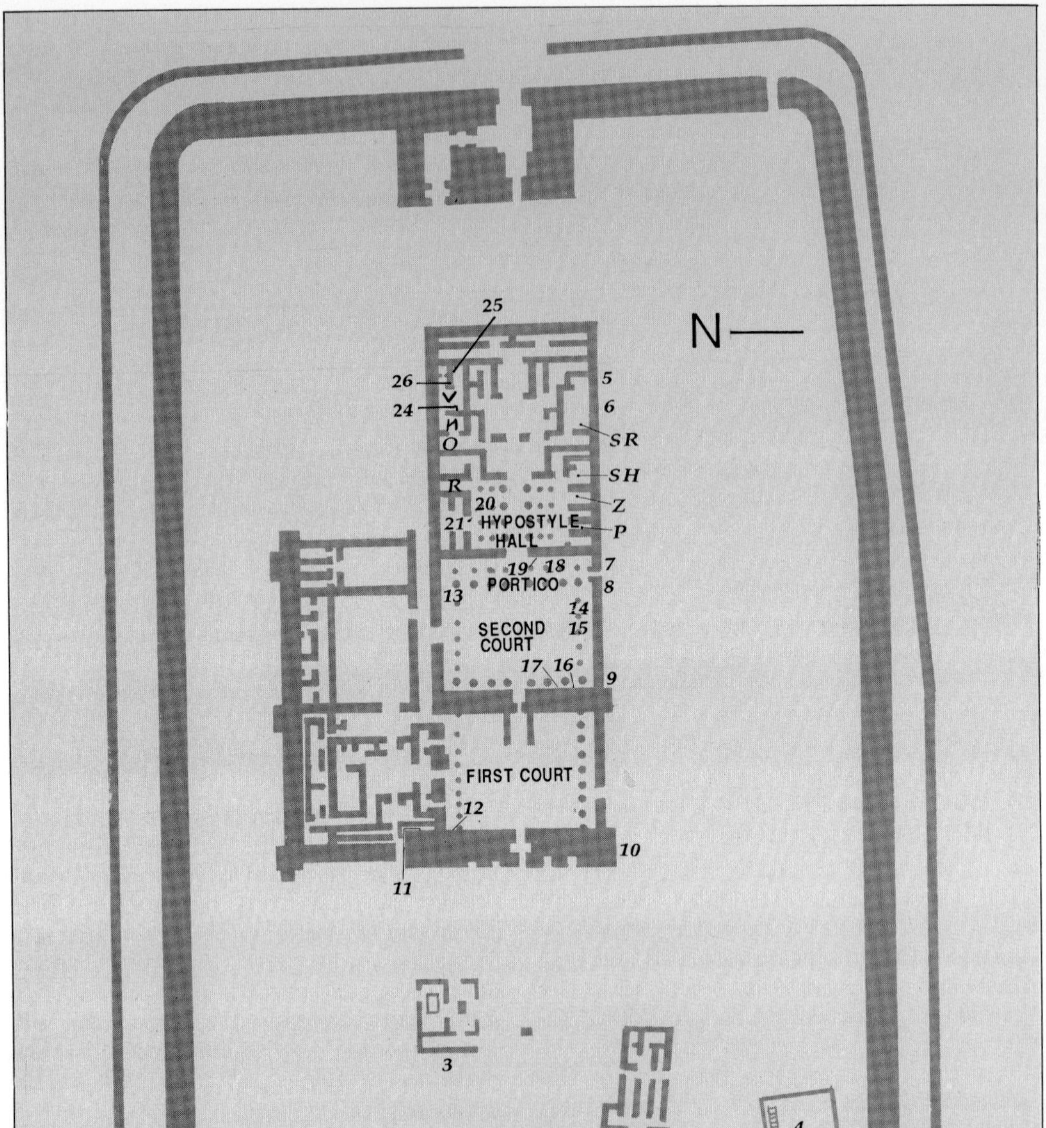

PLAN OF THE TEMPLES OF MEDINET HABU

campaigns in the Levant: certainly it presents every appearance of being a defensive structure, with the tower bases sloping away from the walls, and plenty of vantage points, or hides to shoot from (such as those inside the gateway, high on the walls), where the carved busts of captives would hide an archer or two. Ramesses III had private apartments in the upper rooms of this gateway *(unfortunately often closed to visitors)*, from which he might gaze on the crowds below or watch ceremonies in progress; so the gateway was also a kind of pavilion.

The faces of the two towers show the king raising his mace to a bunch of captives. Around the base of each tower, Asian prisoners bound at the elbows, await their fate. The stronghold was the way the temple presented itself to enemies of Egypt and its gods. But the gateway has another aspect, too. On the left, at *1*, a deteriorated relief presents Ptah – patron deity of craftsmen – as an intermediary. Here, at the point beyond which the *hoi polloi* were not permitted, citizens could present their petitions to Ptah, who would intercede on their behalf with the powers within the walls. Notice the nail-holes around the image: they probably supported the frame for a veil. Two statues of the lioness goddess stand guard in the wall niches.

The Grounds

Pass through the gate and walk a little way into the temple precincts. Here, the scale of the endeavour at once becomes apparent. To the right (2) is a small cult temple built by Hatshepsut and Thutmose III (among others); to the left, at 3, a finely engraved shrine to Amenardais, a daughter of the Nubian King Kashta during the Kushite period around 750 BC. In front stands the temple of Ramesses III, and surrounding the whole, the huge black perim-

The great eastern gate at Medinet Habu

eter walls. The site occupies two hundred and fifty thousand square feet and was covered in ancient times with priests' quarters, butcheries, bakeries, a royal palace and a sacred lake for ablutions – the remains of which may be seen east of Hatshepsut's temple at **4**.

Although this was a mortuary temple – with the purpose of sustaining the king in the *Dwat* (or netherworld) – there was hardly a funereal atmosphere about the place. It must have bustled with life: it was a self-contained town of some size.

These buildings are much ruined now. During the Libyan invasions and civil disorders which came with the collapse of the Ramesside dynasty in the eleventh century BC, the temple city was often used as a place of refuge and the depredations of daily abuse over many years did more damage than any attacker. An earthquake caused serious damage around the turn of the first millennium BC. Although the small cult temple remained in use, the detailed provision made by Ramesses III for his mortuary monument must soon have become a dead letter. Nobles and officers of state built tombs inside the grounds, and in the Christian era the second court was converted into a church. Eventually a Coptic town sprang up in the precincts and sprawled over the walls. Most of this was cleared by Egyptologists at the end of the last century, but the remains of a few structures can be seen still perched on the northern perimeter walls.

Pylon and Outer Wall

The temple itself is missing a few courses of stone on the right tower of the pylon, but it still makes a clear and impressive point: here we see gigantic reliefs of the pharaoh, clutching his foes by their topknots and preparing to strike them into oblivion. The wretched enemies, from Asia, Libya and black Africa, are offered to Amun in his familiar human form on the southern tower and appearing as the hawk-headed Re-Harakhte on the northern.

The ease with which gods slipped in and out of each others' bodies should come as no surprise – they are all aspects of the one life force. Re-Harakhte represents the sun reborn in its morning glory and is always shown with the sun-disk on his head. A pylon, like a pyramid or an obelisk, is a totem of the sun. So it is here quite appropriate to emphasise Amun's triumphant solar aspect by presenting him as Re-Harakhte.

The pylon and the outer temple walls show the king as the protector of the land from chaos and confusion. A series of reliefs show Ramesses III doing battle with various foes. (If the sun is too strong for comfortable viewing of the outer walls, similar reliefs appear inside the temple.) Particularly at **5**, there is an encounter with the Libyans, who were always making trouble. Notice at ***6*** *(25 paces from the*

Re Harakhte, usually shown as a hawk with the solar disc on his head, represents the sun reborn each morning and the triumph of royal power

N.W. corner) the king is watching his scribes count severed hands and genitals of the enemy; the presentation of these trophies would move his majesty to reward those who turned them in.

Although the Egyptians routed the Libyans, worse was to come. In 1177 BC, the consequences of one of history's great migrations of the dispossessed reached the shores of the Delta. As fierce plainsmen from the steppes of Asia poured into the Balkans, the residents fled in terror. Some fled to Anatolia, where they overthrew the Hittite empire, but many put to sea, roaming the Mediterranean in search of a new home.

Among them were ancestors of the biblical Philistines, Sardinians, and possibly Etruscans – who eventually fetched up in Italy. Although their origins remain obscure, we know them collectively as the Sea Peoples. They came as colonisers and were determined to settle.

But Egypt had no room for settlers, as the Sea Peoples learned to their cost. At *7 (around the northern door of the Portico)*, we see a fierce encounter between the Egyptians (supported by foreign conscript troops in helmets with knobs on) and the would-be settlers in crown-like headgear. At *8 (left of the portico door)*, Ramesses III stands on the heads of a brace of captives, indicating how utterly they are in his power, while he leads his archers in showering the enemy in their ships with arrows. This scene is unique among temple reliefs in showing a sea battle *(illustration below)*. These reliefs as a whole constitute an invaluable historical record of Egypt during one of history's most confusing periods.

Beneath, bound prisoners are being led away. And at *9 (just N. of the second pylon)*, the pharaoh presents trussed captives to Amun. Here is the culmination of all the fury that has gone before. The pur-

Ramesses III tramples captives as his arrows sow confusion among the Sea Peoples

pose of the king's battles was not only to preserve Egypt, but to uphold the worship of the gods and to preserve inviolate their temples; for the gods and their priesthoods were powers in the land.

Return to the the main pylon, at the eastern end of the temple. Notice the small door in the northern edge of the pylon at ***10***. Here is a staircase leading to the top of the southern tower *(currently closed to visitors)*, where astronomical observations were made.

The priests were highly skilled in the stars and their meanings: on this knowledge depended their ability to predict the flow of the Nile, to regulate the calendar and organise the public year.

Behind the pylon at ***11***, the king hunts bulls in the marshes. The scene is dramatic and the wild landscape has encouraged the artist in an attempt at perspective, as the bulls struggle to escape in the reeds. This scene may have represented an actual bull hunt, but we should bear in mind that bulls were sacred animals, and the king's triumph would infuse him with their power.

The pylon developed as a regular feature of temple design in the New Kingdom; its tapering walls add to the apparent height and recall the pyramids of an earlier age, created as stairways to heaven for the spirit of the dead king. Egypt's official religion was based on worship of the power behind the sun, so it is natural that the form of their monuments should reflect this conviction.

Between the standard-grooves on the north tower a text lauds Ramesses III's victory in war with the Libyans, and on the south Ptah blesses the king and confirms him in his position as chosen of the gods.

Passing through the two towers of the pylon, note the holes on either side which formerly supported the door, and the curious pattern of *ankh*s holding *uas* sceptres – symbols of godhood. The great door would rest here when open.

First Court

This space served both as the entrance to the temple and as forecourt to the royal palace to the south. On the north side, the court is a colonnade with large statues of Ramesses III bearing a crook and a flail – symbols of sovereignty; a small prince and princess stand beside him. Regrettably, the statues were ruined by the Copts who found the heathen images distracting.

On the North and South walls, battle scenes feature the Libyans and Asiatic foes. Captives are presented to the gods on the southern columns. On the inside face of the first pylon *(S. tower at **12**)* Amorites are shown in a vain attempt to defend their fortresses from the invincible warrior king. The inner face of the north tower bears a lengthy description of the battle against the Sea Peoples together with another hand and genital count.

The first court was considered holy ground, but there were degrees of holiness. This area was relatively public and there is little doubt that, on special occasions, people of some degree would have been allowed in. The southern wall, which also formed the front of the now ruined royal palace, is pierced by a large window, formerly with a balcony where the king

Gruesome trophies of a dirty war

The second court of the Temple of Ramesses III

A shaded corner of the first court

would appear to his courtiers, priests and others. For this reason, this area was known as the *Court of Appearances.* The busts of prisoners were probably placed beneath the balcony so the monarch would seem to his admirers to be trampling on the heads of Egypt's foes. A familiar theme. Scenes of festive wrestling appear in the bottom register on either side.

Second Court

Move up into the second court, and closer to the godhead. Here, the magical purpose of the temple becomes clearer. Within the security of the fortress, the mysteries are enacted. The walls of this court act as a mnemonic in stone for the vital ritual acts which sustain the fertility of the land.

In this court, in later times, Copts held their Christian rites. We can be grateful that, this time, they refrained from hacking out their ancestors' reliefs, but contented themselves merely with plastering or painting them over with whitewash, which has preserved most of them for posterity. However, almost all the massive statues of the king as Osiris have again been struck down.

Most reliefs in the court depict scenes from some of the many festivals celebrated by the priests and the king or his representative. There is space here to mention the two most important: that of Sokar-Osiris-Ptah – a kind of seed-time festival; and that of Min – a celebration of the harvest.

Sokar-Osiris-Ptah – usually known as Sokaris – illustrates well the Egyptian penchant for comprehensive magical insurance. These gods were all connected with growth and creation; amalgamated into one, they became an even more potent force. In Egyptian iconography, deities were often shown as aspects of one another. All partook of the one vital principle, but certain ritual statements demanded specific combinations of the gods' powers to render them effective.

(Unlike the deities of classical antiquity, those of the Nile valley had no recognizable personalities: they were not like humans at all. There is no extensive body of legend about the Egyptian pantheon, apart from the Osirian fertility myth. The boundaries of their influence were loosely defined and constantly shifting. They are perhaps best considered as abstract principles of creation and patterns for the human psyche.)

On the main day of the festivities, a gilded statue of the composite god would be carried in a shrine aboard a small boat, decorated at the prow with an ibex head. The scenes in the upper register at **13** and to the east and round the corner show Sokaris being taken from his shrine, put aboard his boat, and sallying forth on the priests' shoulders into the daylight to do the rounds of the perimeter wall where, from behind his veil, he might greet the people.

Not shown here, but an essential part of the associated ritual, was the preparation of small fertility totems in the shape of the mummified Osiris. Seeds would be put in each and they would be sprinkled with water and covered. The 'coffins' would be opened on the main feast day to display the sprouted seed, so symbolising the regenerative power of the life force in the soil. The dolls would then be buried in the fields. It is probable that a bull, representing Osiris, was sacrificed and his blood spilled on the ground. The pharaoh took an active part in all these ceremonies, confirming the special relationship between the living god-king and his fellow deities.

On the north wall, and extending to the inside face of the second pylon, the corresponding festival of Min is shown. The king is depicted at *14* being carried to the shrine of the god, then visiting him in his naos and, beneath, making a sacrifice of many kinds of food.

Min *(see above, pp 17 & 35)* is a fertility god, usually distinguishable by messy chiseling in front of his thighs where his enormous phallus has been gouged out by prudes. At *15,* he is borne on a litter from which lettuces sprout. The lettuce was sacred to Min. Today, many Upper Egyptians will swear to you that eating lettuce will give a man sexual potency, which shows something of the hold of tradition over the popular imagination. Min was officially addressed as *Bull of his Mother.*

Preceding the god's litter is the pharaoh and a white bull, sacred to the god, which would probably also be sacrificed in thanksgiving. Also in the procession are the king's sons, the chief priest and his standard-bearers. At *16 (round the corner on the east wall)* four blue birds are released to bear the news of the successful completion of the rite to the four corners of the world. At *17,* the king is depicted cutting a few ears of emmer-wheat, a symbolic act designed to ensure a safe harvest. He sniffs the ripe wheat, then offers it to Min, whose erection is its totem.

Min borne on his litter

Taken together, the two festivals in praise of Sokaris and Min represent an attempt to ensure that inert matter is invested with the life force through sympathetic magic. Such appropriate acts of propitiation were intended to bring sustenance and protection to Egypt during the year to come. They link humankind with nature using powerful archetypes of the collective unconscious.

Throughout history, Egyptian peasants have remained true to the practices of their ancestors. To this day, at seed-time, fellaheen women of Gurna place in the earth small bags filled with soil and moulded roughly into the shape of a man which contain a few grains of wheat. Being devout Muslims, they utter prayers seeking the blessing of Allah on their crop.

Those who work the fields along the Nile know (perhaps better than we) that cultivating the right attitude to the abundance of nature is a vital part of cultivating the crop itself, as seed-time ripens to harvest, and the miraculous cycle is repeated, year after year.

Portico

A portico covers the west side of the court. The west wall shows Ramesses, accompanied by his sons, facing the door to the inner parts of the temple. The principal prince wears a long, see-through skirt to show his elevated position. The others make do with the more conventional, shorter kilts.

The murals behind this shady colonnade are rich with much of their original colour. At *18* (between the second and third pillars), Seth and Horus anoint Ramesses III with a stream of *ankh*-crosses, symbolising long life. On the other side of the doorway, the monarch pays his respects to the Theban triad and to Montu of Armant (the original god of his tribe) and Atum, representing the creation principle.

The portraits of the king on each side of the doorway at *19* would have been particularly elaborate. Nail holes show where garments done in precious metals or stones would have been hung about his person. Hieroglyphs here have the king urging us to "be pure!" as we enter this area of his temple denied to all but initiates.

Hypostyle Halls & Inner Temple

Today, there are no hypostyle halls. The columns toppled in the earthquake of 27 BC and were used as quarry for less noble buildings when the area became a Coptic town.

The ground plan and some column stumps remain, however, and we know the interior of the temple must have resembled closely that of Ramesses II, which served as its model.

These parts of the temple would have been dark in their day and well guarded. In the south-east corner of the large hypostyle hall *(room T)* there was the temple's treasury. At *20 (north of the door)* Ramesses III offers booty and captives to Amun.

The reliefs inside this suite of rooms show the king depositing prodigious quantities of gold, silver and precious stones to the account of Amun. Particularly notice the fine workmanship in the presentation scene at *21*, in which Thoth acts as a celestial teller; he is shown weighing the king's latest donation.

The chapels in the first hypostyle hall were home from home for very important visiting deities such as Ptah of Memphis (*P*). There is also a shrine at *R* to the deified Ramesses II, the necropolitan neighbour whom his namesake most admired.

Room *Z* holds a now headless mummiform figure of Ptah done in alabaster and holding the royal *uas* sceptre combined with a *djed* pillar – the symbol of resurrection. It was probably removed from the ruined mortuary temple of Amenhotep III nearby.

The **'Slaughterhouse'** at *SH* should not be visited by sensitive vegetarians. It contains a detailed cartoon cook-book of *ancienne cuisine* for the tables of the resident deities, showing how to do bulls to death and chop them up for offerings. It is unlikely, however, that the killing took place here; the space was too restricted. There was no ceiling to the room, so it may have served as a kind of barbecue kitchen.

The **Solar Rooms** at *SR* were dedicated to Re-Harakhte, the god reborn in the morning. The passage of the sun through the night was a symbol for the journey of the soul in the underworld. The scenes here serve a similar purpose to those from the *Book of What is in the Dwat* on royal tomb walls.

Most are in fairly bad condition, but a clear tableau remains on the architrave at *22*, where the king adores the solar barge, along with eight baboons, cult animals of this god of the rising sun *(photograph on p. 94)*.

The portico

A chant inscribed on the wall at **26** *(behind the architrave)* reads:

The baboons announce Re when he is born
at the third morning hour
They stand up for him when he arrives...
They dance for him; they sing, they clap,
they shriek for him
When this great god rises
in the eyes of his subjects
The people of the sun hear the jubilant
noise of those dwelling in the desert *
Who acclaim the triumphant Re
That he may give life,
prosperity and health
to the king of the two lands, Ramesses III.

*the baboons

Directly opposite the solar rooms, along the west wall, a well-preserved set of rooms *(O and to the east)* constitutes a small temple within a temple. It is the Suite of Osiris. These chambers, like those of Re-Harakhte by the opposite wall, deal with the king's resurrection. But whereas Re-Harakhte is lord of the solar future, Osiris is king of the Fields of Reeds and is shown in that state here.

Originally this temple-chapel had six rooms; however, the outer room (*O*) was later subdivided rather inexpertly by the addition of a small closet, possibly a store for sacred cult objects. The east wall of the first room is devoted to a representation of the king enthroned *(south-east corner)*. Behind him, his mortuary temple is personified as a female spirit. (Since, obviously, the Egyptians did not think the temple resembled this being in any physical sense, it is tiresome to note how literally many commentators interpret the icons of the gods).

The next room (*H*) is a little hall with two columns. There is a number of formal presentations to the more important deities, followed *(south wall)* by the king's coronation in the afterworld. Ramesses kneels before the latent power within the earth – Sokaris – while the principle of royalty, Horus, places a special coronation mitre (the *Atef* crown) on his head.

Baboons adore the Sun, born in the morning

Room *v* probably served as a vestibule for presenting offerings to the shade of the king. The three wall niches at *24* may have contained miniature *djed* pillars. These Egyptian maypoles were sacred to Osiris, and were erected as part of the seed-sowing ceremony. They represent the return of life to dead matter. Between the niches, the king's head sprouts from three *djed* pillars.

Two doorways lead off to the west. That on the right has a vaulted ceiling with astronomical figures which would serve to orient the king in his journey through the cosmos. A false door at the end of the chamber would allow his spirit to pass into the beyond. At *25*, the king offers incense to Min (damaged), seeking the god's aid in prevailing over the darkness of the earth. On the opposite wall, a similar plea is made to Osiris.

The other doorway on the west wall of the vestibule brings us at last, with the king, to the Fields of Reeds. The pharaoh undertakes his ritual duty conscientiously. We see him at *26* ploughing with a team of oxen and harvesting the ripened grain. He adores an enthroned Nile god (with hanging breast and papyrus crown), while a blue heron, representing the abundant inundation, looks on.

Above this tableau, the king is shown paddling past a number of primæval gods and goddesses – principles of material creation – to whom he pays his last respects. Below, his barque travels through the underworld.

On the facing wall, Ramesses presents himself to Osiris. According to the accompanying text, he describes the perilous journey he has undertaken to meet the lord of shadows. The pharaoh puts on a brave front as he proceeds to demand eternal board and lodging from his host.

The inner chamber shows the resurrected king as hierarch – master of the secret forces of the universe. These are represented here by a bull, seven cows, four oars and a number of dour-faced mummies. We cannot hope to discover the true significance of these arcane symbols. It is likely that this mystery-within-a-mystery remained a close secret passed down from pharaoh to pharaoh. Perhaps, in this cosmic game of chinese whispers, even the pharaohs got it wrong.

But carved deep into the sandstone of the north wall, the triumphal words from the *Book of the Dead* proclaim across three thousand years a clear and hopeful message: the mortal king is dead: long live the king!

I recognise I am among the lakes in the Fields of Offering.
Here I am strong, I am full of glory,
Here I exist!
I plough the fields, I reap the fields,
I am fruitful.
Here I remember.
I do not forget.
I am alive!

Ramesses III in the Fields of Reeds

Afterword

Oh, do not ask 'What is it?'
Let us go and make our visit.
– T.S. Eliot: The Love Song of J. Alfred Prufrock

The monuments of Luxor present images and ideas that seem quite remote to twentieth century eyes. Yet, as we have seen, the religious beliefs of many in our own culture relate clearly to models developed anciently along the Nile.

Dynastic Egypt in turn grew out of tribal African society which had existed for countless thousands of years in intimate symbiosis with its environment. But conditions changed; hunter-gatherers settled down and ploughed the fertile borders of the Nile. They channelled the river and discovered the benefits of cooperative endeavour on a large scale. They taught themselves to cast pottery on which they impressed the symbols of their new-found sense of separateness from nature. They invented history.

As they learned to summon forth and regulate the bounty of the earth, the Egyptians began to apply and exploit their capacity for abstract thought. Thus, long before the Bronze Age, civilisation burst forth, complex and adventurous, in the world's first nation state. Eighteenth dynasty Thebes represents a pinnacle of this achievement.

The Egyptians' compulsion to set down their beliefs for eternity has left us a challenging record of their life and thought on tomb and temple walls. We have seen how they built upon their primitive ancestors' intimate knowledge of the natural world to transform their temples into a meticulously detailed ideal universe. They catalogued and calculated and showed things as they ought to be, as well as how they were.

In coming to terms with nature, the Egyptians created an interior world of their own that mirrored reality (even in the New Kingdom, paradise was set in model countryside along the Nile). Their perfected order was not so very different from the natural world which they honoured in their philosophy – they were too close to the land to lose their way in such a vital matter. They recognised their dependence upon the power within creation.

But a capacity for rational differentiation combined with their new technical skills to bring about significant changes in the Egyptians' mentality. The monumental testament of Thebes bears witness to humankind's coming of age but points to the loss of its innocence.

Western society has now built over the Egyptian foundation of natural science and developed it out of all proportion. There are those among us who have abandoned respect for the created universe and for the life within. It is widely believed that we are, in some significant sense, independent of nature.

Through our abuse of rational inquiry we have conjured up the means to destroy our world. Our technical wizardry has developed its own maniacal momentum. A debased consumer-culture, electronically projected everywhere, smothers our spirit. Entrenched technology ensures for us such material control over the natural world that we have been able to construct an almost entirely artificial environment: our sense of wonder seems reserved only for the works of humankind. We have stopped our ears to the harmony of the seasons and made man the measure of all things.

And yet, in every generation, artists and scientists rediscover ancient Egypt; fascinated, they return to drink from the wellsprings of their cultural forebears. In the Egypt of antiquity, we may yet gather some food for thought; some vestiges of reverence for god-in-nature and god-in-man.